D0983874

The Present Christ

The Present Christ

Further Steps in Meditation

JOHN MAIN OSB

Crossroad • New York

1991
The Crossroad Publishing Company
370 Lexington Avenue, New York, N.Y. 10017

Printed in the United States of America

Library of Congress Cataloging-in-Publication Data

Main, John, O.S.B.
  The present Christ.
  "Bibliography of John Main's writings": p.
  1. Contemplation   I. Title
BV5091.C7M28 1986   248.3′4   86-4210

ISBN 0-8245-0740-1

Contents

How to Meditate

Sit down. Sit still and upright. Close your eyes lightly. Sit
relaxed but alert. Silently, interiorly begin to say a single word.
We recommend the prayer-phrase 'maranatha'. Recite it as
four syllables of equal length. Listen to it as you say it, gently
but continuously. Do not think or imagine anything – spiritual
or otherwise. If thoughts and images come, these are distractions at the time of meditation, so keep returning to simply
saying the word. Meditate each morning and evening for
between twenty and thirty minutes.

Addresses of two meditation centres:

Christian Meditation Centre
29 Campden Hill Road
London W8 7DX
England

The Benedictine Priory
1475 Pine Avenue West
Montreal H3G 1B3
Canada

Introduction

An experiential theology

Not long ago I received a letter from a Carthusian monastery asking for more of the books of John Main to pursue the interest excited there by reading *Word into Silence*. A few weeks later they wrote again to express their great sense of discovery. It reminded me of an incident Father John related about the response to his talk on prayer to a Trappist community in Ireland. The abbot had surprised him with a request for an hour's conference on contemplative prayer and he had been led into a gaunt church filled with two rows of silent, hooded monks. He spoke, as increasingly he did in his last years, without notes and from the heart. At the end of his conference the monks filed out silently, without any indication of their response. But just before he left he was approached by an old monk, in his eighties, who whispered his question, 'What was the mantra you gave?' Father John told him, 'Maranatha'. The old man absorbed it for a few moments. Then, as he moved away, he looked at Father John and said, 'You know, I have been waiting for this for forty years.'

To those who heard him pass on the tradition of Christian meditation, John Main's personal presence and authority were powerful reinforcements of the ancient teaching. To Father John himself, an incident such as the awakening of the old monk testified only to the authority of the teaching itself. The medium of communication or persuasion was not his human personality but the Spirit of Christ equally present in speaker and hearer and in the living word that connected them. He spoke and wrote, of course, with the authority of one who had himself been led into the tradition and who had appropriated it within his personal experience. But it was not his own experience *per se* he was trying to communicate. 'In your own experi-

1

ence' was a Pauline phrase he used emphatically in his oral and written teaching. He had supreme confidence in the teaching itself to do the work of persuasion. Cassian's *experientia magistra* (experience is the teacher) expressed a profoundly Christian truth: that Christ is the teaching and the teacher, and that if we can faithfully meet the time-tested spiritual conditions – silence, stillness and simplicity – we will be led into the experience of this unity. 'The first task of the human teacher', John Main would say, 'is to phase himself out as quickly as possible and to lead people to see Christ as the teacher.'

There is then a strong emphasis on experience in John Main's teaching. He restrained the temptation to develop a speculative theology or a teaching that would always be trying to find something new to say. His imaginative intelligence would have allowed him to follow this path. But his own experience – based on his daily meditation – was too real to allow him to forget his personal discovery that Christian prayer is about participatory knowledge, not thought. Seeking only experience, however, could not be the way. In much of the confusion and eclecticism of modern 'spirituality' he saw the dangers of hunting for experience and so of making prayer an experience of inflated self-consciousness. 'If anything happens during your meditation, ignore it. Say your mantra.' This uncompromisingly pure rendering of the teaching would lead to the experience of the Kingdom that cannot be observed. His emphasis on experience carried no dangers of the new gnosticism or the old dualistic pietism, precisely because of this demand of faith. Experience by itself could indeed lead to spiritual anarchy, but experience attended in faith active in love manifests us as citizens of the Kingdom.

John Main, as one of his recent theological commentators has remarked, was not a systematic theologian.* But he was a theologian in the sense of Evagrius' definition: one who truly prays is a theologian; a theologian is one who truly prays. And theology implies some form or system by which both our experience and our understanding of its meaning can be expressed in a way useful and comprehensible to others. To

---

* F. Gérard, 'John Main: A Trinitarian Mystic,' in *Monastic Studies*, No. 15, Montreal 1984.

read John Main's writings, like listening to his tape-recorded talks, impresses one with the inner coherence of his teaching. What is this coherence? The experience of discovering the answer will be the inspiration intended by John Main to lead you into the experience of the pilgrimage. Being given the answer is not the same as finding it for yourself.

However, having said this it is difficult not to suggest my own perception of the pattern, in the hope that it may encourage another person's encounter with the teaching. Certain themes inevitably recur and recombine throughout John Main's writings, from *Word into Silence* to this, the second collection of his 'newsletters'. The coherence of these themes is better sensed when you remember that the context of his writing was always an attempt to communicate experience more directly than we usually associate with the book form. Often his books took shape from talks he gave, and so they deliberately retain as much of the flavour of the spoken word as the medium allows. In the letters sent from the Montreal monastery to a growing number of recipients around the world between 1977 and his death in 1982, there is *teaching*, it is true, but there is also *news* of the community in which this teaching first found expression and which was the human family in which the experience behind the teaching unfolded. Each of these twenty-four letters, the last twelve of which form this volume, represent in modern form an ancient tradition among Christians of writing to each other about their interior experience of Christ and their communal experience of discipleship. St Paul's letters are the pattern for this tradition, but most Christian theology in the early centuries saw the light through the same medium. Where faith and experience are strongest, the highest theology is the least academic. Letters are the most personal form of written communication.

So, the form of these letters itself carries a teaching: the experience *can* be shared, *must* be shared, and the sharing of it creates the community which is, both in its widest and most immediate sense, the Church. John Main loved and respected the Church in its institutional form. But he still saw the Church essentially as an event both personal and organic, and this event was for him the *tradition*, the passing on of the Good News, the transmission of the timeless Spirit which will continue until the end of time. Everything that advances this primary purpose of the Church is therefore traditional. However novel something may seem at first, if it is 'of God', time will show it as being a contemporary restatement of an ancient form, or rather, as being another form of a perennial Christian reality.

As the Montreal community developed we sensed the emergence of this traditional identity. As our own community traditions and customs developed we sensed a rediscovery of an energy which is both form and spirit. Curiously, given our urban setting and small numbers, it became clearer that the traditional model on which we were being formed was not medieval but primitive monasticism. This reinforced John Main's own perception that the most purely traditional is the most radically innovative, because it has restored conscious contact with its roots. It was in John Cassian (a fifth-century monk whose *Conferences* had a formative influence on Western spirituality) that he had found the clearest expression of what we, as twentieth-century monks, were doing. Tradition, in this perspective, becomes not a brake on progress but the rails on which we run the straightest course in the evolution of Christian life and teaching.

John Main's letters began to form a tradition of their own within the larger tradition of epistolary theology. From the first two-page letter written at Christmas 1977, to his last teaching on death before his own death in December 1982, Father John developed a simple format of news and teaching. The teaching section usually followed the news and often was related to one of the news items: a meeting he had had, a development in the community, a new member joining or one leaving. He resisted a proposal to make the format more like that of a conventional community newsletter. To the last the letter was typed on ordinary paper, and he personally wrote the salutation 'My dearest Friends' and signed it. Circulation was about three thousand at the time of his last letter, and, as we sent them out, we were encouraged by the thought that everyone of that number had asked to be on the mailing list.

Tradition and personal experience, Church and society, meditation and prayer: these are the themes you will find weaving in and out of these letters. At the centre is the experience of awakening, of spiritual vision. But it is not just one experience among others in the theological system; it is the controlling experience which encompasses and unifies all the rest. John Main does not try to describe 'what it is like'. For him the experience of the Kingdom, like leaven in the dough, permeates every dimension of living, solitary and relational. One senses this pervasive presence in these letters, written from a vision of the 'new creation' of Christ, full of hope and prophetic encouragement. These twelve letters convey the development of his later theology while his vision of 'Christ in all' was becoming sharper and purer. Anyone who reads them in conjunction with *Letters from the Heart* will sense this growth and feel swept along with it.

The rest of this introduction is meant only to give some pointers to the way into this movement and some of the background from which the letters were written.

A monastic chronicle

Monastic communities like other kinds of families are aware of themselves as passing through time. They also possess the human instinct to record their growth and development and to protect their most significant experiences from distortion or oblivion. The early experiences of a young family, though perhaps the most mundane of its life, are also the most precious and memorable. Meaning always seems most lucid at the beginning.

It may appear conceited or naive of us to feel that the daily life of our new monastic community and its points of growth should be of more interest to people than any other community history. One family photograph album is much like another. Yet hundreds of people who received these newsletters wrote back expressing their interest in the 'news-items' and often asked for more. Perhaps it was the fact that the demand made by the spiritual teaching seemed more humanly possible in the context of the realities of redecoration, individual comings and goings, talks and visitors, guests and additions to the community. This was not just trivia; it was a sign of Christian realism – a sign, too, that what was being passed on in the teaching was not just thought, but experience. The combination of news and teaching made the letters part of a tradition.

In his Introduction to *Letters from the Heart* John Main

describes the genesis of the community. After five years as Headmaster of an American monastic high school he had returned to his own monastery in London to start a lay community based on meditation. He took this step because of a growing sense of failure in monastic schools (most monasteries in Britain and America run schools as their principal work) to provide a truly Christian preparation for life. They sent out well-educated and sophisticated young men who would have a better chance than most of being successful in business or the professions, but 'would they know life in the dimension of Spirit, as a mystery rooted in the joy of being? Or would their contact with life be restricted to the sense of a struggle for success to which the fading memory of their monastic schooling would become increasingly irrelevant' (p. 7).

In writing this he had in the back of his mind the integral spiritual–social role played by Buddhist monasticism in the East. In Malaya he had seen how the young would naturally spend an often prolonged period of spiritual training in a monastery before starting their careers in the world. It is significant that right at the beginning of his experiment in the 'new monasticism' John Main was thinking of the young – the focal point of hope in any society. He sensed a great potential for monasticism in contemporary society and urged this extension, though with little success, on his fellow monks. At first he tried to draw the new, vigorous monasticism he sensed out of the old and tired forms. The lay-community he started in the monastery in London was exceptionally observant of the monastic spirit and daily horarium. Its members lived in a house where silence was practised, television was renounced and they meditated three times daily before walking over to the church to sing the Divine Office with the monks who were coming back from classrooms or parish visiting.

Out of this small community of six laymen living together for six months came the meditation groups that started to meet weekly at the house. These drew in people from outside and generated a need for teaching material in book and tape form.

When news of these developments reached Montreal it evoked an invitation to start a similar venture there. This was an attractive prospect, offering an opportunity for unrestricted development of John Main's monastic vision of a contemplative community forming an intense and revitalizing element in the spiritual life of the local church.

The stages by which this eventually came about are described in *Letters from the Heart*. The passage of time since then has given us a clearer perspective on the conjunction of themes as well as circumstances that led John Main to Montréal: contemplative teaching, monastic tradition, ecclesial need.

In April 1976 John Main was at Gethsemani, Thomas Merton's monastery in Kentucky. He had been invited to give three conferences to the community on 'Prayer in the Tradition of John Cassian'. The transcripts of these talks became his first published teaching on meditation, *Christian Meditation: The Gethsemani Talks* (2nd edn, Montreal, 1983). While at Gethsemani he spent time in Merton's hermitage and wrote from there to a friend: 'I have just celebrated the most loving mass of my life in Merton's little chapel. My purpose in coming here was to talk to the community about prayer, but in fact I have learnt so much myself while I have been here.'*

It was a turning point in his own life; his first major public teaching on the tradition of Christian meditation brought to him an awareness of the purpose for which his life had been a preparation. From there he went straight to Montreal, at the invitation of Bishop Leonard Crowley – for whom he was to develop the highest regard as one who served the Kingdom before all else – and he decided that here was the place to begin afresh. It was also, as we are seeing in hindsight, a turning point or new unfolding of the tradition of Christian meditation. He began his own teaching at the point where another monastic prophet, Thomas Merton, had been cut short, and he would address a great part of the audience whose spiritual attention Merton had gained. He wrote less than Merton, and his teaching was more specific.

In September 1977 John Main and I flew to Montreal to establish its first monastic community. A small meditation group was already meeting weekly at a church in the city, and was using tapes of John Main's talks. So, although we were otherwise unknown there at least Father John's voice had already been heard. After some delay we moved into a house

---

* Cf. My article 'John Main's Monastic Adventure', in *Monastic Studies*, No. 15, Montreal 1984.

on Avenue de Vendôme, which Bishop Crowley had acquired for us, just before Christmas. By then, two of the London lay community had come over to join us. The groups started to meet at the house almost immediately, and they developed rapidly.

Many people asked us why we had come to French-speaking Quebec when so many anglophone Canadians were leaving. That social context was a challenge to our faith in the venture. It never deterred us, and in fact the anomaly of the situation may have actually strengthened our sense of calling to that particular place. However, guests came from way beyond Quebec, many of them coming from the extended community of oblates and meditation groups that has grown up over the years in many cities around the world. Again, seen in retrospect, the choice of this particular city has increased in significance. It is a vital and culturally conscious city, large enough to be international, small enough, in its two cultural groupings, to be human. It is French and English, European and Anglo-Saxon, and is influenced but not overwhelmed by its American neighbour. As a meeting-point of the old and new world it makes an ideal place to renew an old tradition.

The events of the community's growth from 1977 to 1980 are told in *Letters from the Heart*. The present book picks up the story and carries it through to John Main's death.

Almost from the time of our arrival in Montreal we had felt the need for a larger house. The lay community rented an apartment near our monastery, and women guests had to stay in a neighbouring convent. We were receiving an increasing number of long-term guests, including monks and monastic candidates. As yet no novices had been received, although three young men had asked about coming to join us in the autumn of 1980. Every new site we looked at turned out to be either unavailable or too expensive. Then, out of the blue, one of our regular meditators, who had heard of our search, told us of a house his family owned in the centre of the city which might suit us. We were doubtful of this because we needed space and silence and were looking at places outside the city. However, when he showed us the house we realized that Providence was guiding our steps. It was an eighteen-bedroom house with a coachhouse, set in three acres of garden on the slopes of Mount Royal Park, a few minutes from the city centre and yet secluded and silent. By the time of my ordination in June 1980, the house, along with its contents, had been offered to us as a gift by the McConnell family whose home it had been.

My ordination took place in the motherhouse of the Congregation of Notre Dame, who had been very helpful to us in our early days. Their large chapel was filled with oblates and friends of the community, priests of the diocese, and Benedictine and Trappist monks from neighbouring monasteries. It was a symbol of the roots we had sunk and a sign of growth for the future.

Shortly before we left Vendôme on 3 November, we received His Holiness the Dalai Lama at the monastery for the midday Office and meditation, and to lunch afterward. Father John had earlier welcomed him as a fellow-monk at an inter-faith service in the cathedral presided over by the Archbishop of Montreal. In the simpler surroundings of the Vendôme house we shared a deep silence and sense of unity. There is, seen in retrospect, a fitting kind of symmetry to the visit of this Buddhist spiritual leader. Thirty years earlier, John (then Douglas) Main had learned to meditate, as a Christian, with a Hindu teacher, Swami Satyananda, in Malaya. When he became a monk he was told to give up what seemed to his novice master an 'eastern' practice. But then some years later, after enduring the 'spiritual desert' that had ensued, he had rediscovered the mantra in the *Conferences* of John Cassian as being entirely within the Western tradition. Because of the transparent sanctity of his first teacher John Main had never felt threatened by the great spiritual traditions of the East. His own rootedness in the Christian faith was unshakeable and could only be deepened by encountering the self-revelation of God in other religions. So often when Eastern religious leaders come to meditate with Westerners the method followed is taught from the Hindu or Buddhist faith. Now a Buddhist leader had come to share in the depth and silence of a Christian contemplative path, and the unity thus experienced was the more inspiring for all precisely because of that.

Our contact with missionary orders was increasing during this time. John Main had been to Ireland in the summer of 1980 to give retreats to missionaries, Benedictines and Dominicans, and later to monks in the United States. His retreats were always an introduction to meditation in practice as well as theory: the retreatants would meditate together for two or three half-hour periods. These retreats altered the course of many lives.

The larger capacity of our new house saw the expansion of the regular Monday (introductory) and Tuesday (ongoing) evening groups.* There were always guests with us, and many returned home to start small meditation groups on the model of those they had participated in while at the Priory. The simple format of the meeting – talk, meditation, discussion – lends itself to a meditation group in any parish, college, community or home. Every meditator comes, in time, to sense the need for the personal support and encouragement of others on this faith-demanding pilgrimage. It is from this spiritual need that groups have come into being in many parts of the world, and in their development have provided an inspiring model of the Church. These groups have not been initiated from the Priory, but they look back to it as a focal point of the spiritual family of which they now sense themselves to be a part. As they grow, through their experience of the faith-filled presence of their silence, they become not self-serving but other-centred communities of the gospel. The monks who came to form the Priory have, in recent years, also discovered that community is created in the silence of their prayer together. Such a community becomes a hologram of the Church: a part of it, but in that part containing the whole Presence of Christ. They thus revitalize its members' sense of what it means to be a member of the Church as well as what it means to be sharers of the Word. Each group is a cell of Christian teaching; it enters into the presence of the teacher, it consolidates, and its members develop each other's faith.

In Montreal the community integrates its four daily periods of meditation with the Divine Office and Mass. In preparing for meditation – St Benedict's 'pure prayer' – with and by the Office, we feel we have recovered a more traditional sense of the Office as a communal *Lectio* (spiritual reading) rather than as an obligatory act of worship. When we have young people staying with us who have little or no religious formation, it often impresses us how enthusiastically they respond to the Office, which so many priests and religious find a burden rather

---

* The chapters of *Moment of Christ* are drawn from these talks.

than refreshment. Similarly with the Eucharist; in celebrating Mass four times a week rather than daily we avoid the danger of institutionalizing it as a routine. However deep or reverent one's faith, mechanical responses can accrue and deaden the innate sense of wonder and mystery which we need to make the liturgy not only worshipful but instructive. With this schedule everyone in the community looks forward to the Eucharist with an appreciation of its being a gift rather than a right. The half-hour of meditation after communion not only ensures the reverent enactment of the rites but also clarifies the mystery of the Mass as a sacrament, signifying externally the reality of the indwelling Spirit and, in so doing, forming the participants into the Body of Christ's Spirit.

Many of the meditation groups around the world have been started by oblates of the monastery. As a form of association with a monastic community, oblation is as old as Christian monasticism itself. From the days of our first oblates we realized that this form of lay association with our monastery was unusually strong and creative, because of the depth of the spiritual bond created in meditation. Our oblates associated themselves with us for real and personally important reasons, growing directly out of their own spiritual discipline. They share the pilgrimage with us and, as part of their pilgrimage is communicating it to others, they share in our work and often take imaginative initiatives.

Numbering about three hundred and extending across North America, Europe, Australia and Africa, this fellowship of oblates brings together eighteen and eighty-year-olds, conservatives and liberals, laity and clergy. As they share in the experience of the Spirit in our daily life, it becomes for us all an exciting manifestation of what Christian community truly is.

For several years, on Saturday mornings, a group of children has been meeting at the Priory for meditation. This has reinforced our conviction that meditation is indeed 'for everyone' and that the problems we find in learning to meditate later in life would be much lessened if we were taught earlier.

Although most of the teaching at the monastery takes place at the weekly groups and in the liturgy, there are also visits from special groups. Among these are groups of theology students who often express their concern about the absence of a practical spiritual training in their studies. Father John was

11

once asked to give a series of meditation group meetings at the Faculty of Religious Studies at McGill University. I remember one session during which an ambulance siren sounded during the meditation period. The theology professor who had come with his class asked the obvious question: during this time of prayer shouldn't we have stopped saying the mantra and instead prayed for the person being taken to hospital? Father John's response was that in a real sense we were doing this by saying the mantra, because we were entering the Spirit, the prayer of Jesus, who is the one mediator for all. The practical simplicity of meditation opens up a theology of much-needed spiritual depth.

At the heart of this extended fellowship of meditation, united by the 'Communitas' tapes and the newsletters as well as by personal visits, is the monastic community. Now numbering eight, it has grown through the usual trials and tests of all growth. Two of the novices who came into the new house with us in 1980 left within a few months. But their place was taken by others, some of whom came in different capacities, like the former Anglican bishop of Ontario, who became a resident ecumenical oblate and now pursues his work for Christian unity throughout the world.

Other events in the life of our community, from the summer of 1980 to December 1982, are indicated briefly in the opening section of each chapter; these are summaries of the 'news items' which preceded the teaching part of Father John's letters.

Father John continued to speak to the Monday and Tuesday night groups until about six weeks before his death on 30 December 1982. His last teaching letter, of 8 December and the short foreword for *Moment of Christ*, which he wrote during those weeks, speak with an authority and clarity for which his whole life had been a preparation. He used to say we must live well as a preparation for dying well.

To be with him as he died, during those months, was an experience of the transformation of flesh into spirit. In the expansion of the community and the work into which he breathed his spirit, Father John lives more fully than ever, because he lives no longer but Christ lives in him.

1

Silence of Real Knowledge

Among those coming to visit and share our life during the summer of 1980 were an increasing number asking about a monastic vocation.

Father John spoke on meditation at a wide variety of gatherings in Montreal and the United States, mirroring the many dimensions of community life that were manifesting themselves.

The ordination of Brother Laurence Freeman was a milestone in the development of community. The motherhouse of the Congregation of Notre Dame was needed to receive the large numbers who attended – symbolizing what had been achieved and what was yet to come.

One of the challenges we all face is to be continually sensitive to the unfolding of God's plan in our lives: to give free and open assent to the destiny his love is shaping for us. It is so easy to lose that sensitivity. So much of our life is dominated by the mechanical, by the response that is expected or demanded of us, by attempts to predict or anticipate growth, that we are always in danger of losing contact with life as a mystery – and so with life itself. When we cease to respond to life with wonder we begin to understand it merely as a problem, a series of complicated interlocking processes. But our life is whole. And the wholeness is both its mystery and its simplicity.

The wholeness of our life is the harmony of our experience, both its inner harmony, the inner sense it persuades us it has, and the harmony with which it resonates, its reality stretching far beyond the frontiers of our limited experience; the reality which we come in time humbly to realize contains our experience. Experience, though, does not become significant experience, our life does not become charged with meaning, until it begins to repeat itself. The meaning and inner purposefulness of our life usually reveals itself in the pattern of our experience; every pattern is the projection of creative repetition. But of course the pattern is never completed. At least, it can only be said to be complete within the infinite space of God's inner expansion, where all is both new and familiar – eternity. Any fixed pattern we try to impose on our life falsifies the truth of the mystery that is eternally present and so unpredictable. Rigidity is an attempt to evade the challenge our life constantly places before us to remain continually open to the unfolding of our destiny. It is fear of the expanding interiority of truth that tempts us into trying to protect the ground gained rather than pushing the frontiers further, to self-cultivation rather than selfless exploration. Our insensitivity to the mystery of life can wrap itself around us like a strangling vine, stifling the circulation of our spirit and making us ever more closed in upon an examination of our own pain. In the outward circumstances of our life this lingering spiritual death is manifested in the diminishing returns of our attempts at self-distraction, in the deepening fear of boredom. The kingdom of the ego is a grey world without laughter.

If we live merely within the perspective of a fixed pattern, from day to day, we are wasting our deepest response to life on what is passing away. We have not engaged with life on the level at which things endure. To remain thus unaware of the eternal that unfolds itself within our lives out of our inmost being, is the saddest fate that can befall anyone. And the great Christian insight is that this is a fate that need have no power over us. 'Fear not, for I have overcome the world.' Whatever else befalls us the divine perspective can be a redeeming reality for us because all possible human experience, all reality, has been shot through with Christ's redeeming love. We are each of us called to know within this perspective, to be ourselves wholly penetrated with his consciousness, and we are so called simply because we are human and our destiny is to become fully human.

Our gift of spiritual knowledge, our capacity to know by participation, is our gift of life. Whatever our experience may be, it recalls us to the grounding realization that we are and, in contacting this ground of our being – the consciousness that we simply are – we are filled with joy: and the consciousness that Being is Joy once more transforms the pattern of our experience. 'Though our outward humanity is in decay, day by day we are inwardly renewed' (2 Cor. 4:16). Each time we meditate we return to this grounding consciousness of Being, and each time we return to the changing pattern of our life more firmly rooted in our being and so more able to perceive life as mystery and to communicate this perception in joy to others. Our ability to see this is itself the gift of our creation – the gift that is being given with ever-increasing generosity moment by moment. Our creation is ever expanding in harmony with the overflowing love occurring in the secret depths of the Father's timeless mystery. As his being fills our being, our heart is purified and we are led deeper into the vision of God that is his own infinitely generous self-knowledge.

This gift of vision is the wonder of our creation. The perspective with which we are empowered to see is the reality within which we live and move and have our being. It is not a gift we possess but one that we receive and, in returning, receive again more fully. That is why, however long we have been meditating, we meditate without demands and without expectation. Thus the knowledge that God has created us to share in takes possession of us – in a way without our knowing it, yet the consciousness we gain is complete as the self-consciousness we lose could never be. We live no longer but Christ lives fully in us.

Christ is light. He is the light that gives range and depth to our vision. He is also, in his fully realized human consciousness, the eyes with which we see the Father in the divine perspective. Without his light our vision would be tied to the partial dimension and our spirit could not soar above itself into the infinite liberty and crystal clarity of the unified state. Our consciousness would, however wonderful, remain an observer on the periphery of his space, unfulfilled by union with his consciousness, unco-ordinated with his Body. Without his Spirit dwelling in our mortal bodies and opening up the infinite dimension within our spirit, we would be like men restricted by their own innate limitations from moving freely in the liberty they have been given. But the light that transforms our weakness, that makes our limitations the crucible in which his power is brought to perfection, has been freely given, poured into our heart as the pure effulgence of the Father, for Christ is the radiance of the Father. The light we need to empower our vision is not less than this radiance, the glory of God itself. 'For the same God who said, "Out of darkness let light shine," has caused his light to shine within us, to give us the light of revelation – the revelation of the glory of God in the face of Jesus Christ' (2 Cor. 4:6).

For those of us humbly treading the pilgrimage of prayer into this experience of light this is the only fundamental knowledge we need. It is the word that summons us out of the fixed pattern and inspires us to align ourselves on the expanding reality, to place our centre of consciousness beyond the limits of our own self-preoccupation and to discover that our centre is in God. How any of us come to begin this journey is not so important as that we do in fact begin. To begin, it is only necessary to enter into one moment of commitment – one chink in the wall of the ego allows in the light that will flow in more and more powerfully and will steadily overcome all that prevents complete translucence. This moment of commitment is always upon us. It is never an absent ideal, a future possibility but always a present reality. The only question is whether we are sufficiently present to ourselves to be able to see it, to hear the invitation and respond. Every moment is the moment because all time has been charged with divine meaning. Our age is the age of Christ, the age of the glory of God, and it awaits the completion of its transformation by our awakening, our realization. 'Now is the acceptable time.'

Our day-to-day life is of vital importance, as this mystery of transformation is worked out in us and through us by the power of Christ. No detail is insignificant if it is seen in the true light because the reassimilation of all creation in Christ is to be complete. And so our hours of prayer are of supreme importance within the continuous expansion of the mystery, if our spirit is to expand in harmony with it and receive the life and light it offers us. Nothing should be allowed to retard this process of expansion or to obscure the power of the light. Indeed, nothing can, except our own heedlessness.

The besetting fault of Christians in every age is that they become so busy about so many things that they forget that only 'one thing is necessary': to be one as he is One. The plan being worked out in the life of each of us is the same as that being realized in all creation, the bringing into unity with Christ of all that is. It is a unity that lies beyond our capacity to describe. No part of us is left outside the final mystery of oneness. This oneness is at the same time the primal simplicity of being, the unrefracted consciousness of innocence, and the highest point of evolutionary creation, the omega point that is the genesis of infinite growth. We do not, however, need to be able to describe or even understand this mystery in which our own deepest life-process and inner meaning is rooted. All we need is to have begun to experience this plan as a fully personal reality in our own heart, to have known our creation in its dimension of mystery and to have rejoiced in this knowledge of the One who is One.

We will then have begun to know, and our daily meditation will confirm and deepen the knowledge, that the first sphere of this great movement into unity is the achievement of wholeness within ourselves. As the mantra roots itself in our being it gently but surely draws all the distracted and scattered parts of our being together. It calms and disciplines the unruliness of our mind, the tree filled with the chattering monkeys. It takes us beyond our self-centred attachment to our own moods and feelings, beyond all desire including spiritual desire. It takes us too through the turbulent periods in which our unconscious fears or anxieties are run off, often disappearing for ever without our knowing what they were. Through all this the mantra leads us into the discipline that allows us to be silent – and it is in the silence that our spirit naturally expands. From day to day also our inner confidence in the reality of our own being is deepened and the fear that we are slipping into non-being or that we do not exist at all, which are the besetting fears of our time, are exorcised. The unfolding of our own harmony is the experience of wonder and beauty that allows us to recognize the wonder and beauty of all creation. The wonder is that we are becoming fully conscious of our own creation, knowing that we are being brought to completion. Yet we are not as it were witnesses at our own creation. We are at one with our creator and the uncovering of our own harmony serves to set up a resonance with the source of all harmony. To find our own centre is the reverse of becoming self-centred. It is to awaken to the centre beyond ourselves, whence we are created and to which we return with Christ, the centre where we find ourselves and him in that experience of communion we call the Kingdom.

I spend much of my time talking with good people who would agree with this at the level of theory and yet are often reluctant to set out on the pilgrimage that realizes it in practice. The ideas and the language we use to express them can become so intoxicating in themselves that they make the pilgrimage, in its wonderful but relentless ordinariness, seem by contrast very mundane. Our distracted need for novelty is better satisfied by the wares of the spiritual supermarket than by the simple labour asked of us in the garden of our daily meditation. We need to be recalled to the practical simplicity of the way in which the mystery of life is made real for us, or rather perhaps how we are made real in the mystery. We are recalled in so many ways it is difficult to understand how the tradition that teaches us this simplicity is so often read, preached and lectured on and yet so rarely followed. The teaching of every major Christian source points to the same set of simple truths: our way into the mystery of life is the way of becoming centred in God, the way of prayer. For John Cassian it was prayer as the way of poverty, a becoming 'grandly poor' in the utter simplicity of the single verse. For the *Cloud of Unknowing*, too, it is prayer as a journey of progressive simplification, a going beyond all words and thoughts in the stark simplicity of the one little word. It seems to me more and more that any talking about prayer that does not recognize that the talking must come to an end and the practice of it begin soon has little value in leading us into the actual experience of the mystery. The gospel itself lies across our theorizing paths at every turn with its implacable injunction to 'become as little children'. In the mantra we have a means that is at one with our end: a way that is simple and absolute. Our daily fidelity to meditation and our fidelity to the mantra throughout the meditation is the sign that we have heard and attended the gospel's call. Each day that rests on the twin pillars of the morning and evening meditation is a step on the pilgrimage from theory into reality, from idea into experience as we turn aside from all complexity, all trivial concerns, simply to be one in Him, with Him and through Him.

The silence releases the power of the glory of God in our heart. Indeed we find the silence itself as a power within us, the power of the Spirit who in silence is loving to all, and the silence we find through the poverty of our mantra. As we approach that profound silence reigning in our heart that is the Spirit, we know that it is itself the light, the glory that beckons us onwards. And as we pass more fully into the transforming aura of this silence the greater becomes our wonder, the deeper our joy that we are on this pilgrimage at all.

There are days in our lives, days of epiphany, when the unfolding revelation takes on a wholly incarnate form and the plan of the mystery is made visible. On such days what seems the toil and labour of the pilgrimage gives way to enfleshed grace. The centre of the pattern dilates and touches us with a sureness beyond the power of any pattern of words or experience to contain. Such a day for our Community was June the 8th, 1980, the Feast of Corpus Christi, the Body of Christ, when Laurence Freeman was ordained to the sacred priesthood.

Understanding can only emerge from within if we begin by accepting that there are many things we cannot understand or can at least apprehend only very dimly. The deepest Christian experience can only be entered upon when the wisdom of this humility has dawned upon us, because only then are we in a position to allow the mind of Christ full realization in our consciousness. Only then can we understand that we know the Father only by means of our union with Christ. Only thus can we 'know it though it is beyond knowledge'. The power of the sacraments is such an area where we can know fully only if we know with him and through him, allowing him to know us. We can talk of the Body of Christ. We can talk of the Priesthood of Christ, but our talk can never plumb the depth of the mystery for it cannot take us into the vision of that divine perspective that is opened up by silence.

Our own intimate involvement and participation in God's self-revelation fills us with an awe that demands silence as the truest and most natural response. It is such a deep involvement that the mystery is closer to us than our own words and ideas about it. It is not simply that God is drawing us closer to himself by the revelation of his plan, it is rather that in Christ we are participating in the eternal meaning of the communion of love that is God. Man is not meant to be a mere onlooker at this mystery. When the Creator, on the ceiling of the Sistine Chapel, passes his life into Adam he looks into his inmost depths and from them he receives man's awakened recognition. God knows himself in man – not as we might hear the echo of our voice in a hollow chamber, but in the full wonder and liberty of his own being. The full flow of the divine current is earthed in man and it fills him with the brilliance and beauty of the Spirit itself.

The sacraments are dynamic manifestations of the 'joy of Being' earthed in man; and so they continually remind us, through the ordinary fabric of our experience, that our potential is to be wholly transfigured by the power of God passing through us and bringing us to the fullness of our creation.

The great moments in which our minds and hearts advance into this fullness are always moments of silence. The moment of silence in the ordination ceremony is the actual sacramental moment of power when we allow all that our words and rituals have prepared us to receive to dilate in the sacred space in which we have gathered and to fill us. It is a still moment, full of energy, the loving energy of God delighting in the realization of his plan for those he has called. In the stillness we are filled with a reverential fear, but it is a fear that flows into supreme confidence in the presence of him who discloses himself to us in love. Everyone present is turned in the same direction, drawn and at the same time liberated by the power that unveils a reality encompassing the bishop, the priests, the new priest and everyone assisting but that goes beyond all into the mystery of God in whom space and time subsist. It is one of those moments of transcendence when we are taken beyond ourselves and yet are never more truly the person we are called to be.

The sacrament of Holy Orders, like all sacraments, is an outward sign, a sign of an inner reality that is pure openness to God and the power of his love. In the generosity of that openness there comes an end to all the barriers preventing the free flow of that power. The knowledge of the reality of the universal communion that his love ensures expands, and we know that all things are held together by love. Because this is the inner dynamic of the sacrament we celebrated with Bishop Crowley in the Chapel of the mother house of the Congregation de Notre Dame here in Montreal it is no idle thing to say that all our friends were there with us, as Laurence was led deeper into the mystery of creation.

Every life is charged with meaning from within. Every

pattern we try to impose on our experience from outside inevitably falsifies the truth. This is the dangerous quality of language, for whatever we say about the mystery of God expanding in our life, or of meditation itself, misses the wholeness of the truth and usually its simplicity. One aspect of the mystery usually gets ignored or distorted as we talk about another. In talking of meditation as the way we lose our life, go beyond our self-consciousness into the clear light and open space of Christ's consciousness, we often distract attention from the profound degree to which we find our life, discover the unique and abiding gift of our own being in its union with God. We talk too of silence as the natural medium in which this discovery is made, but in talking of it we suggest that it is a negative value, the privation of sound and image. That is why the experience of silence is so vital for any right understanding of it. Only in entering the mystery of silence in meditation can we understand that, though it certainly demands faith and discipline, it is the silence of love, of unqualified and unconditional acceptance. It is the silence which proceeds from the overcoming of time and space; limiting patterns of the mind dissolve when all has been said and understanding has begun to flourish in communion.

To begin to understand this from our own experience it is only necessary that we begin to commit ourselves to it as the truth. Confirmation then follows our commitment. In the external features of our life we begin to see reality in the perspective that only centrality (being rooted in our centre) can give. Our vision, our understanding, expands from within this centre where our mind rests in silence in meditation. Let your mind rest in the heart, say the Upanishads. Set your mind on the kingdom before everything else and all else will be given to you as well, says the Gospel. The fact that we are, in our most real being, rooted in the silence of this centre seems to us the most elusive truth of our life. But the problem is our distractedness, our possessiveness. In fact the Spirit waits patiently for us in its own eternal stillness. Our pilgrimage of meditation teaches us that in spirit and in truth we are there already, with our Father who has called us to be there, who created us to be there and who loves us to be there.

Our awakening to this reality is the expansion of our spirit. With expansion comes liberty, the liberty of spirit that pushes forward the range of our limited consciousness by union with the human consciousness of Jesus dwelling with the infinite space of his love in our human heart. Yet there he dwells with the most perfect respect for our freedom, for the destiny being shaped for us in the bosom of his Father and our Father. The liberty is our capacity to enter with undivided consciousness into this destiny and to know it as the perfection of the mystery of love. This knowledge is not theory or speculation but contact with the most immediate and personal reality. We are not meditating long before our eyes begin to open upon epiphanies of love in our life that before we were too short-sighted to perceive or not generous enough to receive.

The mystery of faith is that liberty is the fruit of rootedness. Our materialistic, egocentric values dispute this, seeing freedom as the absence of commitment, freedom *from* ties or responsibilities. This is the negative protection temporarily offered by the ego as it demands the fruit before the flower. But while our ego is being melted away and our desire dissolved in the faithfulness of our meditation the kingdom dawns. The mantra leads us into the rootedness that bears fruit beyond our imagining. Through all the directions of our pilgrimage the simple faith of our single word keeps us homed on our only destination, the only destination there is, the unshakeable reality of the Father's love. There we enter upon the infinite expansion of heart that liberates us once for all from all narrowness, all insensitivity, all the shadows of the ego.

Our language will only frustrate us unless it leads us back into the refining silence. This is why it has to be a language of opposites, trying to be truthful to the freshness and eternal simplicity of the paradoxes in which we see our spirit expand beyond the fixed patterns. But the mind cannot know this as a separate reality, to analyse, remember, quantify. The mind is itself transformed by this knowledge – the knowledge proceeding from the heart's silence that only the heart can know at source. The knowledge of love is only knowable in love's transformation. Our mind finds its peace through being still in the heart, and in that union of our own being we awaken to a greater union still of which this is but a sacrament – the union of all in Christ who transforms all by the grace and power of his union with our Father.

2

Absolute Gift

In the summer of 1980 we were offered a large house and estate which wonderfully answered our needs. The house stands in three acres of wooded garden on the slopes of Mount Royal, only a few minutes from central Montreal. Four young men had recently come to be novices at the Priory – this giving a special sense of providential design to the move.

Our guests included several missionaries en route to or from their assignments. Meditating with them reinforced our conviction that the way of meditation is a way for all walks of life and vocations even, indeed especially, for the more active.

The oblate community continued to expand, with new members from across Canada, the United States and Europe. In Toronto great interest in the work of the Community led to an invitation, from a large network of meditation groups associated with the Priory, to Father John to speak there in November.

During the summer Father John went to Ireland, where he gave meditation-retreats to the Benedictines at Kylemore and the Dominicans in Drogheda. Later he gave a retreat to the Benedictines at St Louis Priory, Missouri.

Shortly before our move from Avenue de Vendôme, we received His Holiness the Dalai Lama, after an inter-faith service at the cathedral. As a fellow monk he meditated with us after the midday Office, and at lunch he presented Father John with the traditional white silk scarf of Buddhist esteem.

There is a deep and urgent need in our society to recover the true experience of spirit. By 'true' I mean an experience that is fully personal, really authenticated by the engagement of our whole person. It is not enough to be moved by another's spiritual experience. It is not enough to approach the dimension of spirit merely with part of our being, whether that part is intellectual or emotional. The fullness of the spiritual experience to which we are each summoned requires not less than everything we are.

I would like to put before you an aspect of this conviction which was emphasized for us this summer as we meditated with our missionary guests – men and women who meditate daily through lives of active and often very courageous service, and with the Dalai Lama, spiritual leader of one of the world's oldest and largest contemplative monastic orders.

Meditation, as the way of a life centred faithfully and with discipline on prayer, is our way into this true experience of spirit, of *the* Spirit. As anyone who follows this way soon comes to know for himself, its demand upon us increases with each step we take along the pilgrimage. As our capacity to receive the revelation increases so too does the natural impulse we feel to make our response, our openness, more generous, more unpossessive. The strange and wonderful thing is that this demand is unlike any other demand made upon us. Most demands upon us seem to limit our freedom, but this demand is nothing less than an invitation to enter into full liberty of spirit – the liberty we enjoy when we are turned away from self. What seems the demand for absolute surrender is in fact the opportunity for the infinite realization of our potential. But to understand this we cannot flinch from the fact that the demand is absolute and consequently so must our response be.

So used are we to what is relative rather than absolute, so used are we to making compromises, that it often seems that the absolute response is an ideal rather than a practical possibility. 'It would be nice if we could but it just isn't realistic.' The urgent need facing the Church is to awaken to the fact that not only is it realistic but it is the only way to come into contact with reality. The Church has no less need than the rest of society to recover the true experience of spirit as the central priority in its life if it is to be true to itself, its Lord and its vocation. Only if it has personally recovered this knowledge in lived experience can it point the way forward to the fundamental truth of the human mystery which is the mystery of Christ. The absolute commitment required was described by the early Church as faith – faith in the utter reality of God's revelation in Jesus.

The challenge to the Church is the same one facing all men

and women – to understand that the absolute is the only realism. For those who have begun to awaken to the mystery of Christ it is perhaps easier to understand how practical is the absolute because what they are awakening to is the mystery of the incarnation of the one who says 'I am'. The Spirit dwells in us as absolute gift, unconditionally. It dwells in us in our ordinary humanity, a humanity that is weak, vain or silly, that knows failure, mistakes and false starts. Yet it persists within us with the complete commitment of love. It dwells within us through the humanity of Christ and it is through the mutual openness, the union of our consciousness with his that we are empowered to make that absolute response which is the secret meaning of our creation.

Any life which fails to place this mutual openness, which is prayer, at its centre loses its balance as it moves away from its centre of gravity, and it can only fall into one or either extreme of solemnity or triviality. Between these two extremes is the discipline of seriousness, the truly serious approach to life that prepares and sustains us for the response to the absolute. In that response we enter into the experience of pure joy, the joy of being, the joy that underlies everything we are and everything we do. Beginning the journey of meditation is to begin to understand that it is for this joy that we have to learn to prepare ourselves and that our capacity to receive it with open, generous hearts depends upon the generosity of our discipline.

This is why our response to the absolute reality is a matter of absolute ordinariness. We live in a world where it is the extraordinary, the phenomenal, that fascinates and attracts attention, and this is often manifested most of all among religious people. Underlying this kind of sensationalism and cult of novelty is a loss of faith in the mystery of life as it is given to us, as absolute gift, to live and to live in its fullness. What has been lost is essential to the survival of the contemplative experience at the heart of each human life and of human society – the sense of the wholeness of life. The mystery of life is its wholeness and the wholeness of life is the mystery that continually deepens the perspective of our consciousness.

If meditation seems to people to be an unrealistic, non-incarnational dimension to our spiritual life it can only be because the experience of this mystery of wholeness has been lost or has become merely notional. The truth of the Incarnation is that the absolute reality of God has touched and indeed become One with the variable, contingent reality of man. God became man so that man might become God, as the early Fathers of the Church express it. Staggering as this revelation is and feeble though our capacity may be to receive it, it is all worked out through the ordinariness of our human person and the ordinariness of our human life. And for this reason we meditate as an ordinary reality of our daily life, every morning and every evening. It is part of the routine of our daily life, but unlike the other, largely unconscious parts of that routine our times of meditation are moments of ever deeper wakefulness, ever fuller consciousness.

The growing sense of unreality that is overtaking our society often leads people to an intense self-consciousness about the more mundane routines of life, like diet or exercise. The tendency of such self-consciousness is to spread to every other part of our life and for this reason a hyper self-consciousness about food is not infrequently associated with intense self-consciousness about 'methods of spiritual realization'. The tragedy of this type of self-consciousness is that it has its origin in a loss of the experience of pure consciousness and though it is an attempt to recover that experience it is an attempt doomed by its very nature to be counter-productive. The simple truth is that to enter into undivided consciousness, into purity of heart, we have to leave our self-consciousness behind. He who loves his life will lose it.

There comes a point in time after we have begun to meditate when the self-conscious novelty of it wears thin and the ordinariness of it begins to appear. It is, ironically, at this moment when our self-consciousness is beginning to fade and the experience of wholeness begins to emerge that many people give up. The power needed to continue and to allow the mystery to dilate at the centre of our being is again what we call faith. What the Church has always known is that faith is pure gift. The power that enables us to travel deeper into the ordinariness of meditation is fully personal, calls forth from us a mature acceptance, but it is not our own in any possessive or self-dependent sense. We know it as the faith Jesus himself communicates to us through his consciousness dwelling undividedly within us and among us. We receive this power from this source deep in the centre of our spirit where his Spirit dwells. We receive it too from the word of faith spoken to us in innumerable ways by our fellow men, both saints and sinners, the human community of the faithful.

Hearing the word of faith is to experience a challenge addressed to our whole person to realize our wholeness. It is a challenge we can find many ways of postponing. Our lives are busy, distracted. They are designed by social pressure and indeed by our own fear of stillness to be very busy. How many people, seeing a spare time in their average day or a spare evening in their average week, react automatically by looking for some activity to fill it? Our contemporary conditioning tries to make it second nature for us to believe that if we are not doing something we will cease to be. Our being, we are encouraged to believe, depends on our activity.

It is this delusion that causes us to lose our spiritual centre, both personally and as a society. It is a fundamental inversion of reality. It is *not* necessary to do in order to be. In fact, it is only if we can first learn to be that we become fit for all doing.

The danger of this truth is that it seems abstract and so, by our current values, impractical. It remains, that is to say, what for so many Christians the Gospel can remain – a beautiful theory. In the spiritual life, a life committed to reality, all theories are dangerous because they can so easily become means of keeping our minds busy while the whole person lives at one remove from reality. Theories are either applied idealistically to ordinary life and produce extremism, an inflexible lack of humanity, or they are isolated from ordinary life to produce a destructive sense of alienation and inauthenticity. The fundamental truths of a life lived in reality are discovered through and grounded in our ordinary lives.

Among so many people of all traditions who have lost a living ordinary relationship with the spiritual, an 'ideal' like meditation can seem in just this way true but impractical – something at best to be practised in one's rare spare moments. It is one of the great dangers of religious people that they can feel so at home in their verbal formulas and their rituals that they fail to recognize such an absolutely fundamental value of the spiritual life as silence. The most refreshing and encouraging aspect of the inter-faith service held to greet the Dalai Lama in the cathedral in Montreal was precisely the recognition of this value by several thousand people of different traditions when we meditated together in deep silence for about twenty minutes. It was at the same time an absolute and an ordinary occasion, a realization of unity in spirit.

Our lives are not only busy, they are usually noisy. But if our life is to be charged with meaning, to have depth and to be a true growth in consciousness we have to be rooted in silence, rooted in the spirit, in the mystery whose depth can never be plumbed and whose meaning is found only in the consummation of union. We are each called to enter with wonder into this mystery with our whole being, in the total immediacy of the present moment which is the eternal moment of God. To be touched with this wonder is to be made reverent and so to know in the absolute certainty that belongs to our own experience that the energy of creation, the power of love, dwells in the human heart in silence and in the stillness of pure consciousness. The meaning of our own awakening in this power of creation, the meaning of our being is simply to open our consciousness to its source. The source to which we have awakened is our goal. Every aspect of our life, our leisure or our work, relates directly to this meaning. Nothing in our life is without the significance of this spiritual relation and that is why the greatest sacrilege in any human life is triviality. When we have understood this and committed ourselves to understanding it more deeply an entirely new perception of the essential harmony between Being and Action begins to dawn.

The fundamental aspect of this perception is that the apparent opposition between the two is essentially only verbal. Our thinking classifies and divides but our concrete experience unifies. To be truly open to the spiritual reality, through our ordinary practice of meditation, reveals to us the mystery of God as pure activity. Pure stillness, silence, are not inactive. They are harmonized energy, energy that has reached its highest and destined goal, and in this harmony the power and meaning of all movement is contained. The stillness of God into which we enter through our own stillness is the focal point, the centre and source of all activity. Our own stillness is the divine stillness precisely because our centre is in God. The ordinariness of meditation reveals to us as a lived knowledge what thought alone could never convince us of – that Being is pure Action.

Meditation is in no way isolated from the meaning of our

ordinary activity. Our set times of meditation, our fidelity to
the saying of our mantra from the beginning to the end of
these times, constitute the essence of our activities because
meditation is our realization of Being, of pure action. Meditation is pure activity. It is action in the sense that it is the
positive, purposeful deployment of energy, an ordering and
focusing of all the energies that make up the mystery of our
personhood. It cannot be a merely passive state, because what
is both energetic and still is at the highest point of action,
energy incandescent – consciousness. We know this in very
immediate experience, the experience of persevering in our
journey up the mountainside. The faith demanded of us by the
pilgrimage requires the quite unpassive qualities of courage,
perseverance and commitment.

Meditation is pure action that purifies all our other activities.
It is pure because it is selfless, wholly other-centred. Most
of our activities, our hopes and plans are carried out with a
predominant concern for results, for their material worthwhile-
ness. At its worst this concern is mere self-interest, egoism at
its most intense. But any concern for results, for the fruit of
action, betrays a possessiveness or attachment which disturbs
the harmony of the energies deployed in the activity. In meditating day by day, however, humbly and ordinarily, beginning
our pilgrimage at the point we have received the gift of faith
to begin, wherever that may be, we set out into the mystery of
selfless, other-centred activity. We may indeed begin meditating with a superficial concern for results, trying to estimate
if our investment of time and energy is justified by returns
in knowledge or 'extraordinary' experience. Perhaps anyone
formed by our society is conditioned to begin in this way. But
the ordinary practice of meditation purifies us of this spiritual
materialism, and as we enter into the direct experience of
Being, of pure action, we find all our other activities progressively, radically, purified of egoism. To put this more simply –
because meditation leads us into the experience of love at the
centre of our being, it makes us in our ordinary lives and
relationships more loving persons. Meditation teaches us what
theology alone could not convince us of, that Being is Love.

It is so vital for the redemption of our society from the
constricting and complex self-consciousness into which it has
fallen, that this fully personal knowledge of Being, of Being as

purity of motive, as love, be recovered. It can only be redeemed and restored to whole, other-centred consciousness if enough people enter into the pilgrimage that this knowledge demands. Our society can return to sanity, to wholeness and true consciousness only if enough people within it undertake the journey to reality, to the renunciation of self-consciousness, to love. Only in this way can our life be integrally transformed by the power of love that is the Spirit. Our life is a holistic growth, a movement into a wholeness that is infinitely greater than ourselves and yet that contains and fulfils us. Any such growth must have a centre, and if we could find that centre we would have found both our point of departure and our point of convergence. Where then is this focal point of the whole life, where we find both the spiritual reality from which we come into consciousness and the faith that empowers us to embrace it – the reality in which our consciousness is infinitely expanded because it awakens to the mind of Christ with which it is in a union of love?

We know that in terms of the mystery of our own being this focal point is the heart where we are one in body and spirit. But in terms of our daily, ordinary life it is the centrality of meditation in our day, the two periods of meditation on which every day is balanced. The heart of our ordinary life is prayer. The great wonder and joy of knowing this is that the purity of our meditation, our purity of heart, purifies and unifies all our activity, bringing it all into true harmony, into the dynamic state of other-centredness, into the condition of truly loving service. The selflessness of the mantra progressively liberates us from all self-centredness, profoundly summons us into the mystery of the wholeness of life.

To enter into our wholeness is to enter into our selfhood, and this is to enter into God. It is only in this movement of love that our life can find its true spiritual focus and direction. Only thus can it become a wholehearted service of the Lord of Life.

So let me encourage you with what St Benedict calls 'the support of many brethren' in your daily commitment to this journey. In understanding its ordinariness you will awaken to its absoluteness, and then you will know the infinite enrichment of your whole life that is the work of the liberating power of love. Liberated from self-centredness in order to become ourselves, we are led into the experience of communion in which Being and Action are One, the communion of love that is Spirit, the selfsame Spirit dwelling within each of us. We have only to begin the journey and to remain faithful to our beginning.

3

Preparing for Birth

Preparing for the first Christmas in our new home, the Community was very aware of its own experience of growth, indeed of a second birth. There was little time for self-reflection, however, in the work of settling in and keeping warm in a house that was large and beautiful but not too well insulated. Even amid the bustle of moving-day itself we had all stopped at noon for the usual meditation. Through the busy weeks and months ahead the stillness of these times would underpin our life ever more securely.

The new house soon began to fill up with guests and community members. Evening groups on Mondays and Tuesdays seemed almost immediately to expand to fill the larger room. Many new oblates were received, including one from Germany who was to introduce our work there and translate the books into German. Our first oblate and dear friend, Rosie Lovat, made her final oblation, while sharing with us our last days at Avenue de Vendôme and our first, very active weeks on Pine Avenue.

On 13 December three of our novices received the monastic habit. We rejoiced because they had recognized the place where they are called to live in freedom, to develop it and to communicate it to others.

With all the materialistic pressures involved in Christmas today we can easily think of it as a period of hectic preparation, a day of celebration and a brief aftermath. We can forget that it is more than a feast. It is a season. And like all seasons its essence is a cycle of preparation, achievement and then the incorporation of what has been achieved into the larger season of which it is a part, the season of our life.

As the four-week period of preparation for Christmas draws

to a close and we approach the feast itself I would like you to know that we all wish you much joy and deeper peace as we are led more deeply into the mystery of the Lord's birth. Our period of preparation for celebrating the mystery is itself a joyful time, because there is a quietly deepening understanding of whose birth it is we celebrate and just how eternal an event is involved. Each year, it seems to me, the mystery of this birth becomes greater and yet the greater it grows the closer it seems to come to us. In a society that has lost so much of its capacity for peace and so much of the peacefulness needed to prepare quietly for anything, we run the risk of being left only with the worship of the instantly visible, the immediately possessed, of being left finally only with the dryness of the instantly forgotten. Then a liturgical season of preparation, so much part of the deeper rhythms of our spirit, becomes not just a religious but a psychological anachronism. Yet so much depends upon our being prepared, on our having firsthand experience of being ready. If we are to know the truly spiritual quality of Christmas, the meaning of our celebration and ritual at home or in worshipping communities, we have to know what it means to enter into the space where celebration becomes possible with prepared and peaceful hearts. This is one thing our daily pilgrimage of meditation teaches us from within. On that simple and humble journey we know what it means to make space in our heart, to prepare the heart for its great celebration of life. As we prepare, and as our more materialistic expectations and possessiveness drop away, it dawns on us that the event we are preparing for has preceded us. The great liturgy has begun in spirit and in truth.

So often we have the experience and miss the meaning. Later we can know the hollowness of disappointment at what was merely said or done, the external signs that did not connect us with underlying realities. This is the sad result of being unprepared, of being committed to the superficial. Once, though, we have begun to find our true relation in depth, the whole of our experience becomes pulled into meaningful patterns. It is only necessary for us to prepare our hearts to be prepared for everything.

Perhaps one of the reasons that Christmas can continue to mean so much to us spiritually, despite all the materialism and busyness which accompanies it, is that it continues to remind us of our innocence. Too often, however, our understanding of innocence is romantic rather than Christian. We think of a period of 'lost innocence' and so are filled with that great enemy of maturity, sentimentality, and that great enemy of prayer, nostalgia. In any season the balance and clarity of our spiritual response to life can so easily be disturbed by emotional self-indulgence, by the cultivation or indulgence of an image of self; these are the ways by which we stifle our true sensitivity and capacity for empathy with others. Instead of the game of regretting a lost innocence we are called to realize our present innocence, the potential we have right here and now for a direct response. We must cease trying to limit the mystery to forms contained by ready-made formulae of interpretation, by our attempt to 'make sense out of life', which too often means committing the nonsense of trying to control life by devitalizing it. The true character of innocence, however, is energy, adaptability and a wonder that derives its power from within an expanding mystery. If we could begin to know ourselves as naturally innocent in this actual present, we would be preparing to enter not just into the full experience of the Christmas season but of our whole life.

What does it really mean to know ourselves to be innocent? To answer this I think we have really only to look into our own experience. In a moment of pure sensitivity to beauty, when we are suddenly struck with wonder at the sheer power of love to create a new world, or when we are led, beyond our expectations, to set another's interests before our own – in such ways we have precious insights into the real nature of things and into our own real nature. Our elaborate theories and systems simply crumble before the power of the actual experience, one that is so evident, so simple it defies adequate verbal expression. It can indeed only be communicated by sharing the experience-in-itself. Any description of it alienates it from the authenticity of the present when we try to treat it as observable. Whatever can be observed or objectified in this way is static, and it is the nature of the true, the innocent, to be wholly dynamic. It is in this dimension of innocence, the state of a pure consciousness, an undivided heart, that we know the joy we sometimes call liberty of spirit, when we are realizing our potential for self-transcendence. The exhilaration is to know the goodness of the mystery of life unfolding itself in an infinite generosity through our whole self. We sense then the extraordinary inter-relatedness of the mystery, the way our life is connected intimately with the lives of others and all together woven into the great mystery, extending far beyond our imaginations or intellects, whereby all things are being brought into unity in Christ. These are ineffable glimpses of the supreme reality, of supreme love, but at the same time they are absolutely ordinary. We know that no amount of contrivance or experimentation, no kind of fascination with the out-of-the ordinary could have led us into so natural, so real, so simple and so whole a way of being. It is not so much that we see or understand something new as that we *are* someone new, or rather the old person led mysteriously to completion. Reality is not made, certainly not made by us. To be real is to know in our ordinary lives what philosophers or theologians can make sound difficult or pompous, that to be is to be joyous, because Being is bliss: that to be is to be simple – because Being is ONE.

We know only because we are known. We understand only because we are understood. This is the great Christian insight into the human mystery: 'This is the love I speak of, not our love for God but his love for us in sending his Son.' To be innocent is then only to live in accord with this truth of our being. It is to be able to receive a gift with delight, with generosity and without possessiveness. A child's wonder and happiness at Christmas is very rightly seen as a sacrament of its real meaning. It is with the same simplicity that we should receive the supreme gift we receive in the love of Jesus.

The only problem is of our own making, that the outward sign is so rarely seen for its true meaning and so rarely followed through to its inward reality. At Christmas, as at so many times of our life, we are encouraged to remain at the surface level, and without the challenge to sink our roots deeper into reality we drift discontentedly between desire and disappointment. Our society's infatuation with the new, the novel, keeps us well supplied with objects of desire and with distractions to cope temporarily with disappointment. We need a truly spiritual response to life to be able to escape from this *samsara*, this round of death and rebirth. We need it to be able to make use of the innocence we already possess. Because, although we may have known such moments or periods of truth, though we may have strands of clarity and joy running through our life in the form of relationships or gifts, of creativity or service, too often these are not integrated into the unity of our life. They are not linked to the living centre. If we are not deeply inserted into the reality that sustains us in this centre then we inevitably lack any essential unity. We are parts waiting to be made whole. Only to dare to go beyond the superficial, however, is to encounter in a realm of faith not just a beautiful idea, not a fascinating image, not a reflection of our own self-consciousness but Oneness itself. In that encounter our own essential unity is touched awake and we discover that all is one and we are one with the all within the great, simple truth of Christ – the one who is one with the Father – our Father.

But it is easy to remain convinced of our 'lost innocence'. We can do so for several reasons and so slip into that divided consciousness and self-rejection that are so characteristic of our time. One of the reasons for this condition of sadness, of half-life, is, as I have said, because we are so inclined to live in the past, to look for our emotional or spiritual resources in past experiences instead of taking the risk of leaving the past behind and becoming poor once more in the present. We carry so many of the false riches of the past around with us that we do not have hands free to receive the real, living gifts being offered to us. The past can indeed exert a terrible fascination upon us, conscious and unconscious. It can lure us with the gratification of endless self-reflection. One of the ego's most enervating pleasures is regret. And another, very similar reason for our belief in the 'lost innocence' is our obsession with the future. We can invest ourselves so exclusively in future plans and dreams, imagining what might happen, trying to control what we think should happen. In either case the present, where the real is, where the essence of life and the simple secret of joy await us, goes unnoticed, and so we are closed to the God who is ever NOW.

There is something both absurd and tragic about the consciousness that misses the present moment and drifts rootless in the shadows of past or through the fabrications of the future. Its condition is one of self-alienation, and the longer it remains separated from itself the more tired it becomes, the more exhausted by its imprisonment in the self-reflecting self-consciousness of the ego. I have often thought that what many people identify in themselves (with the terrible inaccuracy of egoism) as guilt, their loss of innocence, is usually not so much the weight of their sin as the oppression of their boredom, their lifelessness. Boredom with self, with others, with the hope that the presence of God unfailingly sets before us as an option within our reach, proceeds from an implosion of spiritual energy that it is precisely the invitation of prayer to reverse. The greatest task the Church faces today is to extend that invitation convincingly and as widely, as universally as her purpose demands, and to present it persuasively as an invitation addressed to every man and woman in the ordinary circumstances of their life. Christmas is the feast of the divine explosion – the love of God revealed in the poverty of Christ.

Loneliness, self-rejection, the boredom that the early monks called 'acedia', these are perhaps the most virulent diseases of the modern world and the ones that pose a social threat as much as a spiritual crisis. Indeed the more we proceed, the more it seems that the crisis of our spiritual life is the great and fundamental crisis of society. If our Christian communities are vital, if they have experienced a present reality of the transcendence of their faith, if they are praying communities rooted in the actual reality of the living Christ, then it is to this crisis that they can and should address themselves. If they lack these essential Christian qualities they will fall prey to the egoism our social conditioning has come to encourage. They will become concerned with their image, their success rate, their numbers, their own psychologies. But these are not the concerns of a Christian community. A Christian community has indeed only one concern – to set its mind upon the Kingdom before all else, and all the rest will be given in the measure needed and the way best suited. To set our minds upon the Kingdom, not just as individuals but as integral parts of a community, that is the simple single-mindedness that best describes our true and present state of innocence.

The authentic Christian response in any situation is to address itself not so much to the symptoms as to the causes. This does not mean we adopt a theoretical charity. On the contrary, our compassion and concern are all the more practical because they are directed by a realistic estimate of the underlying causes. And so, in the alienation, the spiritual and mental suffering of so many around us, we see not economic or socio-

logical cases but human beings of an infinite value and lovable-
ness capable of being restored to their true relation with themselves, with others, with God. It is our belief in the curability
of the disease that has gripped our society that makes our
practice of compassion so faith-filled and our faith so
compassionate. We know, because we ourselves are being
cured, that if the slightest aperture can be made in the wall of
a closed spirit the love of God can enter and work wonders
beyond our imagining.

The Christian's experience of this love working the wonder
of God in his own heart means that he is not offering merely
temporary relief, a panacea or a distraction. He is communicating a diagnosis of life that carries within it the power to
cure, a life-giving word. It is a powerful, an awesome message
and a precious responsibility. We cannot pretend that the cure
does not entail a certain rigour, that the way to freedom does
not lie through commitment, and to absolute freedom through
absolute commitment. We can say that the power of this
process comes from beyond us but has taken up its dwelling in
the human heart and that for every one surrender we can make
in that sacred space we win a thousand victories.

To show the way into this space our communities must be
on the way themselves, travelling into the experience of their
own innocence as epiphanies of the Kingdom. The journey
they have to undertake is from materialism to a new-found
sense of the essential quality of life, its spiritual quality
discovered in its ordinariness; from the boredom of
consumerism to the vitality of our full humanity. The frame of
the journey is the central commitment to prayer that really
brings the community to birth in the first place. Until that is
made, the community is little more than a group waiting to
begin the journey, reading timetables and travel-guides,
discussing routes. But it is a journey that cannot be predicted.
It is one that is made wholly in the present; every day we travel
a little deeper into the fullness of God's presence. Ultimately,
it is a journey we may postpone but not one that we can decide
not to make. It is a simple journey, not an easy one nor a
difficult one. Once begun, there are so many strengths given
to us. It is one that attracts fellow-travellers, the greatest
strength. One who begins alone will be joined by others and
in that mystery of communion the Church is reborn, rekindled

in many quiet corners of the earth. However small the corner, it is born in its fullness because Christ is born there, humble, vulnerable, fully human, and in those very qualities bringing us the fullness of the Father's love. And this is why the authentic Christian community, like Jesus himself, has always had an influence out of all proportion to its size and material power. The Kingdom, realized in the innocence of a community persevering in prayer, may not conquer the world but it can love the world and redeem it by its love.

Generalities, of course, can be great enemies of true religion. Blake was wiser when he spoke of the 'holiness of minute particulars'. The restoration of the world to the experience of its own innocence, to the capacity to delight in the gift of life without attempting to possess it, the achievement of a free-flowing spirit – all this is made real not in the media, not in programmes or courses but in the minute particular of the heart. To begin its realization we have to undertake a work, a daily labour, of preparing our heart, of clearing space within it. This is the simple, humble and above all entirely practical work of our daily meditation. Each morning and evening we make space for the kingdom to expand a little further firstly within us and then through us. And it is our mantra, our faithful and continuous recitation of the mantra, that is the little tool clearing the space that opens to infinity.

One of the fears I most often encounter in people beginning to meditate as a daily pilgrimage is that the journey to their own heart, to this infinite space, may take them into isolation, away from the comfort and familiarity of the known into the unknown. This is an understandable initial fear. To leave behind the superficial is what we often mean by leaving behind the familiar and this can create a sense of emptiness as we become exposed to greater depth and more substantial reality. It takes time for us to adjust to this new sense of belonging, of a new relatedness that seems to set all our relations in a new order. Our coming home can seem like homelessness. Reflect a little this Christmas on the homelessness of the stable at Bethlehem.

In time we realize that in this new experience of innocence, of delight in the gift of life, we are leaving childishness behind and entering into the full maturity that Jesus enjoys in the Father, the fullness of his love that enters and expands within our hearts in the Spirit. It is not only now, at the beginning of the pilgrimage, that we need the human love and inspiration of others. But it is now when we encounter an unfamiliarly wide horizon that we have a special need for the power of community with others. Our openness to them expands our sensitivity in turn to their needs. And as the mantra leads us ever further from self-centredness we turn more generously to others and receive their support in return. Indeed, our love for others is the only truly Christian way of measuring our progress on the pilgrimage of prayer.

To those of you who have recently begun to meditate I would like to send you especially much love and encouragement. The commitment this journey calls from us at first is unfamiliar. It requires faith, perhaps a certain recklessness to begin. But once we have begun, it is the nature of God, the nature of love to sweep us along, teaching us by experience that our commitment is to reality, that our discipline is the springboard to freedom. The fear that the journey is 'away from,' rather than 'towards' is only disproved by experience. This is a journey where ultimately only experience counts. The words or writings of others can add only a little light to the wholly actual, wholly present and wholly personal reality that lives in your heart and in my heart. Miraculously we can enter this experience together and discover communion just where communication seemed to break down.

The journey to our own heart is a journey into every heart. And in the first light of the real we see that this is the communion which is the kingdom Jesus was born to establish and in which he is born again in every human heart to realize. What we have left behind is loneliness, confusion, isolation. What we have found is communion, sureness, love. Our way is simplicity and fidelity. The simplicity of the mantra. Our fidelity to our daily meditation. As we travel this way we are drawn closer together by the same power of love that unites us.

4

Belief and Faith

*After Christmas the coach house on the monastery grounds was
converted into a guest house for women and married couples.
We continued to receive many guests, particularly from Europe,
where groups were continuously forming and multiplying.*

*Bishop Henry Hill, one of our first oblates, resigned from the
Anglican Diocese of Ontario and came to live in the community
as a resident ecumenical oblate.*

As our society becomes increasingly less religious its need for
the authentically spiritual intensifies. As the religious and social
support systems fail, we are faced with the urgency of the
ultimate challenge to the meaning and value of life.

I think this is best expressed in Christian terms as the essential difference between belief and faith. A great deal of ink –
and blood – have been spilled through the Christian centuries
over beliefs. And even today, in an age not of faith but of
scepticism and anxiety, what we believe, or think we believe,
can still be a source of division, estrangement and religious
self-importance. How often though does the violence with
which men assert or defend their beliefs betray an attempt to
convince themselves that they do really believe or that their
beliefs are authentic? The spectre of our actual unbelief can
be so frightening that we can be plunged into extreme, self-
contradictory ways of imposing our beliefs on others rather
than simply, peacefully, living them ourselves. There is another
extreme reaction to the uneasy suspicion we have about our
lack of true conviction – that is, not arrogance but indifference.
Feeling our own inauthenticity we evade it by collapsing into
the emotions it creates, fatalism or egocentric pessimism. But
whatever the extreme, bigotry or lukewarmness, the source is
the fear of the gap between what we believe and what we

41

experience. And we know that, if this gap makes us inauthentic, our message – even if it is the gospel – can convince no one unless it has so convinced us that we are transformed by it.

Wherever this fear of our own unbelief grips the Church then what should be a joyful, tolerant and compassionate community united in celebrating the wonder of a common transcendent experience becomes instead either a lifeless observer of formal routines or an intolerant, pompous agent of repression. From our historical perspective we can look back on a Church that has been both of these. In fact, because of the complex and volatile society we inhabit, we can probably find both extremes of Christian unbelief in different areas of the same Church today.

It is an ever-present danger, because the life-force of the Christian tradition is so precarious, so personal and so delicate. It cannot be compromised or diluted without ceasing to be what it is and becoming instead mere pious wordiness or arrogant religiosity. And yet this life-force that St Paul calls the Spirit – the Spirit we must neither sadden nor stifle – is a power of irresistible joy and peace, if only we allow ourselves to be. If we can only find the way simply to be, ourselves, then this power within us dilates and absorbs us. Then we can become what we can so often and so self-consciously talk of being, apostles of the reality that is Christ, communicators of the living energy of his gospel.

One of the great ironies of history is that men have never been able to institutionalize this energy, because no experience of reality can be known except by direct, spontaneous participation. Yet it is only too easy to codify, formalize and institutionalize the inauthentic experience, the memory of a brief glimpse of reality's light. It is this memory, many times removed from direct experience, that passes into the codified beliefs passed on by societies to successive generations.

This gap between the authentic experience and the received memory can become the chasm between honesty and hypocrisy, and this is a possibility that underlies the religious practice of every tradition. It is the gap, simply, between our credal statements and our experience. In a positive light, this gap is our opportunity for growth and development in reality if we can accept it realistically, which is to say in a spirit of humility. We do, after all, know more than we can prove. This gap exists for us all simply because we are born into a long, rich and complex tradition. But to accept a belief is only ever a first step, not, as the agonizers of doubt have thought, the final one. The tradition conveys beliefs to us almost automatically. It would be difficult to say we could ever *choose* to believe, for example. But if this tradition is a living and truly spiritual one, then it will also demand that these beliefs become realized, become grounded in our own experience. The supreme test of any tradition, of its authenticity, is the degree to which it demands this realization of all those who follow it, and not simply the select or esoteric few. And this is the supreme, ultimate importance of the Christian tradition in human history – that it demands, or rather offers, this personal authentication to all mankind. The Gospel is minimally credal. It is not obsessed with right beliefs and wrong beliefs but advances the uncompromisingly personal truth of its message – because the message is the person of Jesus. He does not call us to believe or to do but, first of all, to be. If in the first place we can be with him, then we are fit for all doing, all believing.

However, in a negative light this gap between belief and experience can become a limbo of unreality that is only too easily institutionalized. It can even attract us in the way un-reality does, because it is well-populated by those who have agreed not to tell the truth to each other – the world of complacent piety or of intolerant self-righteousness. A place of slow dying and protracted suffering, it defends the half-life that masquerades as truth. But there is no reason why anyone should settle for half-life. We are called to fullness of life and that fullness has not to be achieved, but only realized, only accepted. We accept it by entering upon this journey of faith across the gap between belief and experience. And on that journey we are purified in the darkness of faith, beyond belief. We make the transition to the deeper level of reality by letting go of all the words, concepts and images that tie us to memory, to the past. Instead we enter the extraordinary purity of the present moment. Entering humbly, realistically, into the reality of our own incompleteness teaches us the wonder of our capacity for infinite growth. But to be taught we have first to learn to be dispossessed. Blessed are the poor in spirit.

Vast numbers of men and women over the centuries, including whole societies, have affirmed their belief in Jesus and his gospel. Our whole Western culture is permeated by this belief even now that those who do still personally believe are probably in a minority. Why, then, has this not transformed the world? This is a vital question for us to understand, and we can only adequately face it as a society or as a Church if we can face it as personal, accepting our personal responsibility for the authenticity of Christian belief at large. A good part of the answer, I think, is that we have glibly confused belief and faith. We have thought that we could convince others that the Gospel is truth by means of our beliefs alone. Those others we called, significantly, non-believers.

Our beliefs tend to be stronger than our faith if we have not yet understood that faith – unconditional, open-hearted commitment – is the fundamental level of our being and of our participation in the mystery of the Spirit's life. What we call belief is the tip of an iceberg, most of whose substance is invisible. Faith makes up the greater and more essential part of our commitment to the person of Christ – the person who is universally present in the energy of his love for all men, all creation, and who is the invisible reality we celebrate and enflesh in our lives and with our whole being. Faith is the invisible but wholly realistic condition of being that allows us to share in the mystery of Christ's self-communication. As a condition of our being, faith is a power. A power within us that communicates itself to others as it is being set free within our own hearts.

The Letter to the Hebrews describes how it is faith that helps us to perceive that the visible comes forth from the invisible. It is our beliefs that are the visible expressions of our faith, our personal commitment to the person of Jesus. But because they are expressions they find form transiently in words, concepts and images. The sense of inauthenticity that can so often overtake the religious mind is frequently due to the fact that we treat the transient as if it were enduring – we overtax the resources of what is finite and changeable. The forms in which our beliefs exist and in which they are expressed are always in the process of passing away – the mind has here no abiding city; only in the heart can we find the enduring reign of God. Whatever has form, like our beliefs or bodies, is always in transition to a new form. Our beliefs are always seeking new definitions, new words to express themselves. When I studied theology our belief in the Eucharist was summed up in the word 'transubstantiation'. Since then many new words, even words like 'transfinalization' and 'transignification', have been proposed as more apt expressions of the mystery of the Eucharist – a mystery we can experience in faith but never solve in words. As words change, and even as the meaning of words change, so in a sense our beliefs change, develop. The fact that we ourselves are changing, being changed by life, means that our beliefs must similarly grow, mature and become more attuned to the mystery that is greater than they are. But what endures, changes only by becoming more perfectly what it always is, is our faith. It does so pre-eminently in pace with our commitment to meditation, the journey of faith. Because in that commitment, each morning and evening, we acknowledge the absolute priority of faith and do so by repeatedly emptying out of it all that is transient, all that is passing away – all words, ideas and images. The language and creative context of faith is silence. We know from our human relationships how much faith we need to have in a person to be silent with them. We know that our faith in a person is deepened by such silence. This too is the dynamic of our silence in meditation – realizing God's love for us expressed in the love of Jesus, deepening our faith in his love. In this silence we are invited to enter into the enduring reality where Becoming is embraced by Being. What is visible passes away, what is invisible endures.

Because of Jesus and the communication of his Being to us, we know that this reality is no abstract, platonic idea. It is a fully personal, wholly incarnate reality. The person of Jesus is the revelation of the person of God. And the gospel, which is the continuation and extension of his teaching and presence, is the revelation of the priority of the personal over all secondary, institutional forms. The extraordinary discovery that is the goal of each person's pilgrimage is that the ultimate completion of each person is effected in Jesus. We are all made one with him who is one with God. To call this a 'relationship' with Jesus only inadequately expresses the wonder of the union that is being realized in the power of our faith in him and his love for us. It is a relationship with Jesus but it is also a participation in his life at source. The deeper our journey of faith takes us into reality the more evidently it appears that this life is the life of God. That life itself is what we call the Trinity, the explosion of love that is the Being of God, the God who is the ground of all Being. And because God is this infinitely uncontainable energy of love, because he simply is love, he seeks himself beyond himself. In obedience to the dynamic of his own being, he seeks the Other to whom he can give himself, into whom he can empty himself. For Jesus, we are that Other. He has sent the Spirit to dwell in our hearts.

The wonder of this is so overwhelming it must make us humble. But it also makes us confident. It is the personal vocation of each of us to experience this wonder in the immediacy of faith, to share, as St Peter tells us, in the very Being of God. But to experience this wonder we have to let go of all secondary forms and expressions. We have to pass definitively beyond beliefs to faith. In the condition of faith we are drawn into the ever-expanding self-knowledge of God. We know him only with his own self-knowledge. We know ourselves and all others only in him. It is only very inadequately expressed as a relationship. The mutual presence and self-communication that is the love-force of the Trinity transcends difference but does not obliterate distinction. In the same way our relationship with God in Jesus is infinitely greater than the dialogue of two self-contained individuals. There is achieved between us a common consciousness, a single ground of being. And this we call love.

Any of the many mysteries of love that make up this reality and point to it is the fruit of faith rather than belief. With those we love we have a mysterious bond, something so close it is indefinable. It is a mutual commitment to each other's uniqueness and an unconditional acceptance of our inalienable communion. This is how we are loved by God and how we are empowered to return that love within the reality of his own Being. The wonder of love is that it always creates its own universe, transforming the mundane and finite into a world of meaning and mystery radiant everywhere with a light that originates deep within our own spirit. This new creation generated by love is built up into an expanding universe by the power of faith – unconditional commitment to what is real but unseen.

The world desperately needs men and women filled with this faith. It is faith that is both the precondition and the medium for the communication of any personal reality. The Gospel as the ultimate revelation of the personal is, as St Paul expresses it, a way that begins and ends in faith. Perhaps never more than today has the world needed a Church filled with men and women of faith – their 'eyes fixed on Jesus', the Invisible One among us, as the Letter to the Hebrews puts it. If it is to respond to this need the Church must sink its consciousness deeper than its beliefs and into the roots of faith – that is, into the consciousness of Jesus. We can do this only at the bedrock of our being where the pure consciousness of Jesus fills and sustains us. In a real sense Jesus himself is our faith, just as the person we love is really our love.

As a church we are not travel agents handing out brochures to places we have never visited. We are explorers of a country without frontiers, one we discover little by little not to be a place but a person. We are not communicating a script, because we are neither actors nor audience. In harmony with this Person and in the light shed everywhere by the reality of Jesus all roles have been burned away, leaving only persons open to each other in love – this is the Church.

To meditate is to accept this exploration of the universe of God as the supreme meaning and authentication of our live. It is to be rooted in faith – like Abraham obeying the call to go out to a land destined for himself and his heirs and leaving home without knowing where he was to go. After you have been meditating even for a short while you understand that our commitment in faith to this reality is always deepening. There is always the home, the familiar ground of our ideas and plans and dreams, to leave behind us as we move more surely towards the heart of reality.

The price we pay for a gospel of absolute power is absolute commitment. As we sit to meditate each day we encounter and are made one with this power at a level of reality deeper than that of belief – more enduring than that of the images and concepts of belief. And as we rise from meditation to commit ourselves with greater generosity to the responsibilities of our lives, we bring the power of this purer reality into every part of our ordinary life. It is through our meditation that in a real way we put our faith into practice.

We are called to believe in Jesus. But our belief summons us to something greater, to faith in him. Our faith then becomes our potential to resonate with him, to be in harmony with him who is in harmony with God. It is a source of wonder and deep gratitude that we have found the way to place ourselves within this harmony. And the way is the way of the mantra, the harmonic of our faith. It includes our belief but sets us free from all the limitations imposed on us by the images and words of belief. It bridges the gap between belief and experience because it is the bridge of faith, the sacrament of faith. Travelling across that gap, going beyond ourselves as Jesus has gone before us and calls us to follow him, we awaken in the heart of reality, in Jesus, who himself is fully awake within the heart of God.

As we prepare to enter another Lent let us keep one another in our hearts. This is a time of conversion – a time to turn from what is passing away in order to be at one with him who is eternal.

5

The Present Christ

During the spring of 1981 one of the great enrichments of our communal life and theological reflection derived, as usual, from the Benedictine charism of hospitality. Guests came primarily to meditate with us, but they also shared in the manual work of the day and observed the prescribed periods of Lectio *(spiritual reading).*

Bishop Crowley paid us one of his regular and very welcome visits. We knew it was not common for a bishop to understand so sympathetically what a monastery is about. His clear and far-seeing vision of the Church of the future made him not only open to development in the tradition but an agent of change.

Father Laurence visited several meditation groups and communities in England, France and Germany and spent time in Trosly-Breuil, the headquarters of L'Arche, Jean Vanier's communities for mentally handicapped people. In Germany he visited our oblates in Würzburg who have been taking the teaching of meditation into the university there. Returning to Montreal he took over the editorship of Monastic Studies, *a journal of monastic theology and scholarship formerly edited from Mount Saviour Monastery.*

The work of the community was extended into the wider scale of the publishing world through the appearance of Word into Silence *published by Darton Longman and Todd in England and Paulist Press in the States. With 'Communitas' a new medium for the teaching was launched. This is a series of cassettes, ten a year, of talks given by Father John to the weekly meditation groups meeting at the monastery. (The series continues to provide an inspiring record of a great teacher's work week by week.) Out of this, too, came a fuller sense of the extended community that had already, silently, come into being.*

The Present Christ

We celebrated the Easter liturgies of Holy Saturday night here with our resident guests and those who had come to join us from outside. During the Vigil it was made very clear to us in a fresh way how much the mystery of Christ consists in his nearness to us. Whatever is distant is merely strange or foreign, not truly mysterious. If, for example, we objectify something or someone we can always admire it but its essential identity is alienated precisely because we have distanced it so far from ourselves. In relation to it we remain mutually isolated and as a result fundamentally unchanged by what we 'contemplate'. But if, in the presence of the mystery of God, instead of objectifying it, we are humble enough in its proximity to be one with it; if we can allow our being to resonate finely with the mystery, then we ourselves are changed and we enter quite another and more creative mode of being. The agent of all objectification, all distancing and alienation is the ego. It is the subliminal voice in our consciousness that urges us to be separate, even from what we worship or love. The fading of this voice of the tempter is the dawning of the reality which we find as we enter the Kingdom of Heaven. It is a reality we can only discover in union, only through union.

We know something or someone *fully* when we simultaneously experience and understand – that is when subject and object are transcended in full knowledge in the state of union. We can only fully understand the closeness of Christ to us from within this egoless state of union. In other words we can only know him with his own knowledge. The knowledge that is love is something more than what we generally think of as a 'relationship', something more achieved than what we think of as a dialogue, and something more incarnate and tangible than what we consider an 'idea'. The deeply moving symbols of the Vigil bring this home to us by pointing beyond themselves and beyond ourselves to a realm of meaning where not even the profoundest symbol, word or gesture can express the fullness of the reality of Christ – for that is a reality known in a deep understanding so infinitely intimate that it transcends both sign and ego and becomes both personal and universal. When we bless the fire at the beginning of the Vigil we become part of a pre-historic dimension of humanity; appropriately and mysteriously we begin the night's re-enactment of man's redemption with a memorial dating from the dawn of human consciousness. The fire we light burns right into our deepest atavistic memory. And then, in the kindling of the Paschal Candle from this same fire we are returned to the presentness of Christ in all time.

Similarly, when later in the evening around the altar we bless the baptismal water, we recreate a primary symbol of the source of life and consciousness, full of meaning too as an agent of purification and clarification. And by immersing the candle in the water we enact the unique synthesis that has occurred in Christ. We are again transferred from a distant mode of being to an encounter with what is immediate and present. For what the symbols remind us of is that the flame of the Christ consciousness has come to dwell in our hearts – for 'we possess the mind of Christ' (1 Cor. 2:16).

The presentness of Christ to us is, as it were, contained within his presentness in all time. As Christian thinkers have realized from the beginning, the redemptive love of Jesus universalized for mankind on the Cross and occupying the centre of all consciousness through the Resurrection, travels both backwards and forwards through space and time, uniting every human consciousness in him. From this moment, in and out of time, man has been plunged into a radically new way of being within the mystery of God. He has been touched by a ray of reality that has opened his eyes to the ambiance within which he lives and moves and has his being. He is now empowered to be with God in a quite unprecedented way, by participating directly and wholly in the plenitude of God's Being. For one thing, he is absolved from the necessity of regarding this Being as an external reality, an object of his devotional or intellectual interest. And so, man is no longer obliged to objectify his source – an objectification that alienated him from it and that we call 'sin'. Christ's forgiveness of our sin is not the reprieve of a judge but the embrace of a lover. Our redemption is our being brought near – so near, in Christ, that we can no longer focus on God as an external object with the mind's eye but are instead taken beyond all images to be in the presence of the truth, revealed in silence; the eye with which we see is the eye that sees us. Our vision itself is Christ.

We are absolved from the need to objectify God, to talk to him, to appease or petition him. 'Your father knows what your needs are before you ask him.' From that eternal moment when

Jesus awoke to his union with the Father, all humanity has passed out of the stage of its spiritual infancy. In one moment it has evolved into maturity, the 'full stature' of Christ. And that moment is to be found in the centre of our own heart where his spirit dwells, like a seed buried in the ground. Finding that moment is the work of our meditation, a joyful and vitalizing work because we travel to the heart's centre in a faith that knows the moment is already born and born for imperishability. And once we have known this fully, through union and in union, our whole being, life and time is rediscovered, united in the wholeness that is our holiness, and all within this moment.

It is not just that we are absolved from the necessity of considering ourselves and God in a dualistic way. It is that we are summoned not to. The time has come, indeed it is already here, when we are summoned to worship God in spirit and in truth. We cannot persist in the dualism of our spiritual infancy and remain in the truth. The indwelling Spirit of Christ is not just a gift, a special offer, a grace we can accept or decline. It is a reality, the door into the sheepfold. As such it is a summons, an inherent power within our destiny to come to completion. But the wonder is that the summons is a summons made by love and that it educates us to itself with an infinite gentleness.

But the gentleness is purposeful and determined, linked to the movement of all creative energy in creation back to its source. The energy of the Christ-Spirit is unquenchable and so ultimately unavoidable. In the ordinariness of our daily life, it is steadily, wonderfully present to us. There is more than just a symbolic meaning, I think, in the fact that the power of the Resurrection reaches us in the springtime of the year while we are rediscovering all the energies of growth in nature, energies that are also intense and cosmic and yet creative of such delicate marvels of earth's beauty.

The essence of the human condition is that it is a condition of growth in all its aspects. In the measurable aspects of our life the growth is contained within the cycle of birth and decline: we bud, blossom and fade. But the profounder dimensions of our life are not measurable, not conditioned by time or space, and in those the growth is of an infinite potential. For us, as for all life that grows, growth can occur only in union. Like all developing realities, tending towards a destined fulfilment of their being, we need roots to connect us unitively with the source of life's energy. For man, in his essential nature, the root is Christ and the source of life is the Father. Our union with Christ, the mingling of his consciousness with ours at the entirely human level, is the heart of the mystery of our life – the mystery to which all growth, finite and infinite is an awakening. Perhaps the greatest mystery is that even the most finite, the cycle of birth and decline, is fundamentally changed by the power of this union. The Resurrection is the saving of the whole man, heart, mind, spirit and corruptible body. The power of this affirmation of the divineness of the human condition is that the life of the Father flows into us through our rootedness in Christ and the channel of its communication is the human consciousness of Jesus, wholly open to the reality of God and dwelling at one with us and within us. His openness to the Father in his human consciousness is the condition that allows us to realize our union with the Father through him in *our* human consciousness. With him, we travel beyond ourselves, beyond himself into the heart of God – this is transcendence realized.

'All that the Father has is mine,' Jesus told his disciples, and he has revealed to us everything he has heard from the Father (John 15:16; 16:15). It is as a result of this oneness of Father and Son and of the Son's oneness with us that we are able to stand in the truth. The innate restlessness of man in his condition of growth is the consequence of his having an expanding capacity to be in the truth, to be one with the truth. He is impelled by the inner expansiveness of his own being to align himself to his destiny and to enter the simplicity of the egoless state which growth demands – the need to let go of the past and to venture upon what is to come without desire or resistance. We are restless for the truth; above all, the truth of our own being, for there we can be sure we are not encountering an image or theory of truth, but truth incarnate – what we instinctively recognize as reality. The revelation of the Father to us that occurs in union with the consciousness of Jesus is the fundamental authenticity of human life. Without contact with this source of being we remain rootless, meaningless, theoretical and static. Without the touch of truth we stay as imaginary creatures, struggling to make fantasy or intellect substitute for the real. But this is an unbearable, negative restlessness, for the attraction towards the truth is the deepest characteristic of the human spirit. In our innate movement towards the real and the true, we are more deeply in touch with ourselves than in the more superficial (and common) movement towards fantasy. In the centre of our being where, until we travel there, we think we are most closed in upon ourselves, there is an opening towards a wholeness that is infinite, towards God. It is here we encounter the utter simplicity of our contact with truth, where the revelation of the Father becomes actual. The Greek for truth is *alētheia*; it means a revealing, an uncovering. To find the truth we need not images but an open heart.

The mystery of Christ reveals man's new involvement in the truth and it makes us wonderfully, terribly present to God. Even our rituals and symbols cannot distance him who has drawn so near to us. He is God with us, Emmanuel. And yet, if we can learn to be with him, to awaken to union, then his closeness to us is not a source of fear but of peace. 'He himself is our peace' – a peace that is both the fulfilment and harmonization of all creative energy, beyond our ordinary understanding. The harmony is achieved when we have taken the step of faith into the silence in which the truth resides, the step from image to reality. In the marvellous dispensation of God we have only to take the first step for us to be swept along by his power for the rest of the way. That is why we discover that the truth we yearn for is not a cold platonic wisdom but a movement of love. The indwelling of the Spirit of Christ is itself the whole of this movement of life resolved into a Person and it lingers within us with the ache of love until it evokes a fully personal response.

The presentness of Christ to us in this way is our transition from image to reality, from idea to Person. We are the 'heirs of the prophets'. In the new modality of being that has the risen Christ as its definitive and universal centre, all symbols find their resolution. Even the most sacred and potent symbol is only a stage in the revelation of a reality that is already one with us. That is why we are now called to 'worship the Father in spirit and in truth': because in the immediacy of Christ's presence this oneness is manifest. In direct communion 'to be with' is 'to be in love'. An early Christian writer put it very simply: 'Who bows to the statue of the King when the King himself is present?'

I think this is what makes the Christian revelation so mysteriously contemporary in every age, so innately 'modern'. Perhaps what we call the modern consciousness is in fact the Christic consciousness of union, and maybe we first encounter it in the spirit of the pages of the New Testament when Peter, in the portico of Solomon, declares with the irrefutable authority that comes from a transcendent experience 'and so said all the prophets from Samuel onwards; with one voice they all predicted this present time' (Acts 3:24).

The faith of the Christic consciousness contains this extraordinary sense of having reached the fullness of time. When it is repeated as a mere theological formula it inevitably sounds astonishingly arrogant. But spoken out of the experience of the Spirit who inspired the prophets to imagine such a time it becomes mysteriously persuasive and strangely non-controversial. 'All these things that happened to them were symbolic and were recorded for our benefit as a warning. For upon us the fulfilment of the ages has come' (1 Cor. 10:11).

To hear this proclaimed with authority is to be awakened to an unexpected experience – not merely to the presentness of Christ in time and in our own lifetime but also to the fraternity of all mankind that this creates. We recognize our solidarity as men because we stand together, in the same place and in the same time before the same mystery. This is why 'he himself is our peace'.

The sense that we are already at the convergence point for the destined growth of all consciousness in creation back to the Creator is intoxicating. But it carries with it also a profound sense of responsibility. If we are no longer in the infancy of mankind then we are summoned, personally not anonymously, to a maturity of spirit that we often (such is the appeal of the unreal) prefer to postpone rather than realize. But the end of a period of preparation becomes immediately the beginning of a time of perfecting and we are, each of us, summoned to reach this perfection. Our vocation is no less than to be holy – not 'holier than thou' but as holy as God in whose fullness of being we already share (2 Pet. 1:4).

The reality Jesus has uncovered for us is the new age of Presence. It demands a correspondingly new understanding of how we share in the Trinitarian mystery. Because of the new Christic consciousness we can understand in a way that is disturbingly personal and universal, that we do not so much exist in relation to God as subsist within God – he is the ground of our being. We are called to know and to know fully, not just notionally, that nothing can be outside the ground of all Being that God is. And so, in the light of Christ, prayer is not talking-to but being-with.

In the past, recent as well as distant, man has thought of himself as a creature summoned to surrender himself to his Creator. He has been dominated by a sense of the infinite superiority of the divine mystery to himself. This sense of the distance of the untouchable God does not lead us into the experience of transcendence, of being swept out of ourselves, beyond ourselves into the mystery in which we have our being, but rather, so often, it leads into fear of what is so far beyond our control and yet so powerful over us. Man's prayer in this condition of non-growth becomes a psychological means of coping with a fear that is perhaps our most fundamental terror – the fear of ceasing to be. However great our sufferings or disappointments we are always more deeply and chaotically terrified by the prospect of extinction. And, if our knowledge of God stops short at this fear of his power over all being, we can see him only as a threat to our being, our conscious survival. So, our prayer comes to be a way of pleasing or placating him, and in petitioning him we hope to 'turn his anger from us'. But all the time the fear has us in the vice of paralysis.

This is God as Creator. But Jesus opens up God to us as Abba, Father. And, in this most personal yet universal of revelations, our dependence upon God is changed from being a source of terror into a source of infinite joy and wonder. We are because God is. God is our being and so our being is good, as he is. We have nothing to fear of such goodness because of the perfect love that is his goodness; the Trinity's explosive creativity burns away all fear. And so, the ground of man's most haunting fear – of isolation and the extinction to which all isolation leads – is revealed as illusory. The dream-world created by the ego and the source of all our sense of isolation, fear and loneliness, the world that is itself only a terrible mistake, an absurd mis-rendering image of reality, is dissolved by the sheer power of God's love.

Prayer, in the Christian vision of reality, is the way we experience that the basic condition of man is not separateness but communion, *being-with*. This indeed is the Christic consciousness of love, both commanding and empowering us to *be-with* everyone out of the harmony of our own basic experience of communion. 'Love one another as I have loved you.' In giving us his whole self Jesus authenticates this teaching with an absolute and final authority. In the light of this teaching, of this self-giving and of the consciousness that is communicated we can no longer seriously think of ourselves as summoned to 'surrender' to God. In any surrender we retain the human failure to dissolve the illusion of dualism. There remains an I to surrender, a Thou to be surrendered to. And in the light of the reality of God it matters little whether such dualism is retained due to fear or false piety. The result in either case is a kind of spiritual schizophrenia. We cannot surrender to the one with whom we are already united.

But we can awaken to and realize our empathy. In the Christic consciousness, and most urgently for modern man trying to come to terms with this new being, our relationship with the divine has to be understood in terms of empathy.

It is true that to realize this empathy a type of surrender is involved – this is the dynamic process of any experience of love where self is lost in the other. But it is not surrender *to*; it is surrender *of* – the surrender of isolation, fear, possessiveness, self-centredness, all the demons bred in the breeding-ground of the ego. It is the surrender, the letting-go of this reflected self, the false image projected in self-consciousness that we fear. But if we can, even for a moment (the first step of faith), move aside from the distorted field of vision of the ego then we look upon the selflessness of love with unimaginable wonder and excitement. But the knot that seems to hold us is a paradox, a strange compulsion, for we are frightened to lose our fear.

This is evident in a short while to anyone who has begun to meditate. He becomes aware almost simultaneously of the extraordinary new perspective on reality that opens up and of the strange insistence we can have to remain within the narrow world of the ego. But he realizes too that the way forward is the way of poverty. We enter into the freedom of poverty of the mantra. And this is simultaneously the loss of fear and the winning of freedom. It is always difficult to communicate this to people who are not meditating. Yet it has to be communicated. There is a strangely apostolic dynamic in this deep interior poverty of the Christ-spirit. Somehow, as Jesus recognized and commanded, it must be told; and somehow, provided that the poverty is generously enough embraced, it does communicate itself.

The most frequent objection is that this is not what Jesus meant by loss of self or that this is not Christianity but a form of monism. I can only think that if Jesus meant a 'partial loss of self' he would have said so and that the mystery of Jesus is precisely his oneness with God and his oneness with us. But we cannot understand what he meant by saying 'the Father and I are one' unless we can enter into the living experience of our oneness with him. To enter that experience is our prayer and it is an entry into the prayer of Jesus. The koan of the saying, 'the Father and I are one' is unresolvable but it dilates beyond the confines of logic in the experience of the Spirit, the bond of oneness between Father and the Son, the prayer of Jesus, our prayer.

'The Spirit prays within us.' It is this Spirit who is the guarantee of the fundamentally positive dynamic of laying down our life, of leaving self behind. There are other forms of selflessness which are not positive – self-rejection, the abandonment of self to mass-hysteria or anonymous forms of the denial of life. But these are precisely those forms of surrendering-to that only intensify the anguish of isolation. In meditation, on the other hand, we embrace the entire naturalness of the surrender of isolation and we do so in the power of the Spirit of oneness, the Spirit of love. The error we made in the past was that it seemed we had to be thinking about this Spirit if it were to be there to help us. But of course the Spirit is unceasingly present and potent within us and by its silence calls us into its own unified consciousness. The irony is that while we are trying to conjure it up by thinking about it or by imagining what it would be like to experience it, we ourselves are not present to the Spirit. That is why the first step in faith is to stop thinking about God at the time of prayer. We have instead to believe – not just mentally but with the whole of our being that makes belief into faith – that he is with us and we in him. 'Dwell in me as I in you.'

The path of meditation is the path of faith and the sacrament of faith is our silence. The door to silence is the mantra. It is not then long before we begin to understand that the loss of self involved is not abnegation but empathy, not an extinction of individuality but a communion of persons. For as we become more deeply rooted in the ground of our being we have our being clarified and affirmed in the purifying silence of the mystery present to us in our heart.

The power of the Resurrection collects the whole of time and space into a single, universal focus. Within our own hearts a cosmos has also been radically transformed by this same power, brought to the single point of a pure and limitless love. We are no longer outside creation or outside God, because through the power that dwells in the open space in the centre of our being we pass beyond ourselves into his fullness of being. To do this we have to be simple enough to be rooted in reality, and faithful enough to stay on our pilgrimage and to meditate each morning and evening. Then we realize our union with our point of origin. Our destination and our companion are one. 'I call you servants no longer; a servant does not know what his master is about. I have called you friends because I have disclosed to you everything I have heard from my Father.' It this that makes the pilgrimage possible for us all.

6

Sacramental Vision

*Month by month we continued to hear of the ongoing develop-
ment of meditation groups in Toronto and Ottawa. In May,
Father John visited these Canadian centres to meditate with them
and encourage them on the journey.*

*In Montreal we continued to be amazed by the richness and
unpredictability of community. The stroke suffered by one of
our older oblates deepened for us St Benedict's words on the
care of the sick, in whom, he said, we see Christ. Another oblate,
who had come with us from the lay community in England,
married and moved to an apartment near to the monastery. This
was for him the beginning of a dimension of the community that
later developed in physical proximity to the monastery.*

*After conducting visitations and presiding over an abbatial
election in an Irish Benedictine monastery, Father John visited
an old friend, Mgr Tom Fehily, who had begun meditation
groups in Dublin. Returning to Canada he led an important
session on meditation for a large assembly of sisters in eastern
Canada.*

Greetings in the Lord. Today we have been celebrating the
Feast of St Benedict and it seems a suitable date to send this
letter out to so many of you who share with us his vision
and achievement. His understanding of the Christian life as a
commitment to ordinary reality rooted in the contemplative
experience has inspired and continues to inspire people in many
different walks of life and following different vocations to the
one God. I remember some years ago hearing an old monk
quoting a description of monastic generosity that seemed to be
wonderfully apt: 'on things of no account an unaccountable
zeal bestowing'. It is the particular that reveals the universal,
and a commitment to perfection in all we do for its own sake

that enables us to leave ourselves behind. The genius of Benedict's vision is that whereas this approach could so easily become fanatical, he renders it humane, compassionate and tolerant – truly Christian. The enduring power of his vision is its humanity. So often a religious vision of life can lose its human focus, but for Benedict it was through the humanity of Jesus and our own humanity that we enter the divine mystery.

I returned from Ireland in June in time to celebrate Corpus Christi with the Community. Annual feasts like this have an important part in clarifying the Christian rhythm of our life. They can never become routine, because they can never be celebrated in the same way – provided that we have ourselves grown in the interval between the celebrations. Like the Mass itself, the great feasts are expressions of a mystery that we are continually growing into; and so, our outward rites and forms, though remaining the same, are always conveying some deeper, clearer aspect of the mystery. Provided that we are committed to this continuous penetration of the mystery, our rituals can never become routines and the mystery can never become mechanical. A feast like Corpus Christi gives us a regular opportunity to focus, within the liturgical mystery itself, the way our thought and experience have developed. And it does this, as all liturgical action does, by helping us to bring our thought and experience into deeper harmony. This is something we have to be open to, especially in regard to the Eucharist, which focuses our whole religious, sacramental life, as well as providing us with a vital source of the strength we need to remain faithful to the pilgrimage.

The general experience of someone who has been meditating for a while is that the Mass becomes both more meaningful and more of a mystery. This becomes especially clear when, as in this monastery, there is an opportunity to integrate the celebration of Mass with meditation, meditating after the communion. It brings home, in a very powerful way, the true purpose of all the words and rituals we use in worship – not to communicate something *to* God but to prepare ourselves to enter communion *with* him. All religious words point and lead to the silence of a spirit attentive to the presence of God.

The Mass is a supreme symbol of the Christian mystery of Incarnation. It teaches us, in a concrete and tangible form, that reality is incarnate, not conceptual. And it reminds us that it is as we are that we are to make the commitment to this reality – fallible and fickle human beings, redeemed by a power both greater than ourselves and totally committed to us. The extraordinary revelation of the gospel is the absolute value of the ordinary and the potential of the ordinary, to be transfigured by the divine power, the universal energy of love. A life that is structured within the discipline of our morning and evening meditation is rooted in the reality of this power and so is always being transformed and penetrated by it. What we might at first seem to 'lose' by sacrificing the time for meditation in the course of a demanding day, is not worth comparing with what we gain. We indeed *re*gain even what we lose, both because of the sense of clarity and order which meditation gives us in our ordinary decision-making, and because of the sharpened sense of the value of time and our growing incapacity to waste or use it trivially. But above and beyond this, a light is shed on our life and radiates through it, that reveals it in its true meaning and sacredness. Our meditation deepens our appreciation of the Mass because it refines our perception of our own life as a sacrament of the love of God.

Meditation highlights even the most ordinary and routine parts of life and draws out their hidden sacramental value. The source of most discontentedness and frustration is just that this value has been lost to man and, looking at his life and work in search of meaning, he can find nothing but a series of self-referring values turned in upon themselves. The search for meaning is the search for the sacramental nature of the ordinary and immediate. This mysterious nature, the value given to it by its divine origin, is there. It is not our creation. It is not even our own meaning reflected back to us by creation. The things and processes of the world have a meaning, a value of their own and this is why we can be transported by a sense of wonder at the beauty of creation and feel ourselves rendered more meaningful by being part of it. But the direction given to us by our own meaning and purpose points us directly towards the originating centre of all meaning, to the Creator. His reality is absolute because in him, the inherent meaning of all creation is focused and realized. In him, we live and move and have our being. This is why we cannot awaken to God without awakening in wonder and compassion to the reality of mankind, both in general and in the particular persons who are for us the sacraments of God's personal mystery and with whom we turn towards his central presence. The sacramental value of these persons and of all the processes and things of our life lead us back to this Presence. Modern man is so often sad because he thinks this value has been lost. The truth is that neither we nor creation have lost the divine radiance. But we have lost the faculty of seeing it. To be saved is to regain it, and our redemption is achieved because we now see all creation with the vision of Christ and, extraordinary though it may seem, we see more – with the vision of Christ we see into the divine Mystery itself.

St Benedict reminded his followers (in chapter 19 of the Rule), that the divine Presence is everywhere. The maturing of our spirit, in the course of our life, is simply our growth in this capacity to see this Presence in every part of our being and experience. To see it is not possible unless we are prepared to become one with what we see, just as we are one with the power of seeing. Our union with Christ is our way into union with the Father. This process of unification is the deepest mystery of our life and the greatest power in creation. It is detectable only imperfectly and in localized areas. We cannot stand back on a spectator's bench and watch the process at work, because we are not the centre of the process and even our own centre, our objectifying consciousness, is being unified. All this, the process of 'oneing', is the work of the Spirit. It is the Spirit itself, at one with his own work as he is with the Father and the Son, from whom he proceeds. The shape and form of this process varies according to the material with which it is involved, but it is the same Spirit working in all and through all. It is the Spirit crying 'Abba' in our heart and leading us into union with the Father through the Son. It is the Spirit who unites the bread and wine with the body and blood of Christ and who unites those who stand around his altar with each other and with him.

The Spirit is the spirit of God who is love. One of the discoveries made through the experience of love is that we truly find our own innerness in the other and that we ourselves become the temple of their interiority. This is the loss of self-centredness and the restoration to real selfhood in the beloved. Another way of putting it, is to say that the division we assume to be so definite between the inner and outer worlds is simply dissolved, gradually perhaps, but no less surely for being gradual, by the reality of the power of love. The energy we employed to maintain this illusion of dividedness is transformed into the liberty of spirit and joyfulness that characterizes the person 'in love.'

We see reality as divided into inner and outer worlds because we ourselves are divided. The accumulative force of our meditation heals this wound in our consciousness and the effect of healing is to make whole. More and more we are allowed to see reality as a continuous whole and, as we become one with ourselves, we are no longer spectators watching the world and ourselves through cracked spectacles. What is the power that restores us to this sense and knowledge of the wholeness of ourselves and of reality and of the harmony between the self and creation? It is the power of the wholeness itself, the uninterrupted presence of God in all persons and all things. To experience God as Creator is to experience the liberation that every encounter with truth – with things as they really are – provokes. And we know him as Creator and creating, when we encounter reality in our ordinary experience as having a divine centre and meaning. This again means all reality because reality cannot be divided. There is not a 'religious' area of our life where this vision is seen and other areas where it is not. To see it is to see it everywhere. The religious response to life is a response based on wonder and on a sense of the incompleted potential of life as we are living it. As the roots of the word imply, religion *relinks* us to the power that brings life to its destined fullness, which is its wholeness. The different parts of our ordinary experience are then no longer alienated from each other. We are empowered to see one area of our experience in terms of other areas. We see with the vision of God. And we see in both the 'abstract' and 'concrete' manifestations of reality, the same presence of God shining with supreme, benevolent simplicity.

The presence of God can never be a partial revelation of his love. Wherever he is, he is wholly present – unlike man's ability to be only 'half-there', such is man's divided and distracted nature. We know this only too well from the sad experience of being with someone who is evidently not present to us as we are to them; or of ourselves being unable to concentrate on what we are engaged upon. To meditate is to know the value of being able to pay complete attention to whatever we are doing or to whomever we are with. Learning to do this through our simple fidelity to the mantra is a real entry into the sharing in the being of God, which St Peter says is our fundamental call. For God is turned with complete and undivided attention to us in Christ. Wholly turned toward us, he is wholly loving. That is why we do not say just that God is loving but that *God is love*. To be wholly loving is to *be* love.

If God were in any degree self-centred – if he were not wholly attentive and concentrated in his movement of love – then we would be able to analyse, to objectify him, to know him as an external manifestation of reality. Then men would be able to 'see God and live'. But as it is, his *completeness* allows us to know him only by participation in his own self-knowledge, which is itself an ever-flowing stream of self-transcendence, creative *other-centredness*. To enter the life of the Trinity through our union with the Son, is far from settling down to the contemplation of a finished picture. It is to be swept out of the sideroads of our self-centredness into the living stream of God's eternal creative love.

We could never recognize the presence of God in the reality in which we find ourselves if we did not already 'possess' that presence; or, to put it better, if he did not already know himself and us in our human heart. 'The love I speak of is not our love for God but his love for us.' We are touched into consciousness by his presence; his spirit is breathed into us. Then we awaken with a growing wonder, awe and joyful confidence in our own reality to his presence around us. We are incapable of seeing reality until we ourselves are realized, made real by his presence. To know ourselves is to know God in us, to know God is to know ourselves in him. It is this dynamic of growth in consciousness, that is profoundly reciprocal, that underlies the central paradox of the revelation of Jesus – a revelation of the nature of the reality that we find our life in the losing of it. The expansion of the frontiers of our being by our growth into the mind of Christ is a centrifugal process, proceeding from the centre of our being outwards. The way we make this journey 'outwards' is by the 'interior' journey of meditation.

In the Eucharist we have a real and living symbol of the unity of the interior and exterior aspects of reality. But what is the special quality of the 'real presence' of Christ in the

Eucharist? It is not that the presence of God-in-Christ is less real in other dimensions of life. God cannot be more or less present, as he is indivisible; but we can, of course, be more or less open to his Presence due to our dividedness. It is rather that in the Eucharist we meet a fully human sign and realization of Christ's universal presence. We call this manifestation *real* because our grasp of reality is stronger at the level of human encounter; the experience of human love is the necessary first stage for the realization of the true nature of love as God himself. 'The glory of God is man fully alive.' In the Eucharist, we encounter the human love of Jesus, fully humanized and so fully realized and integral with the reality of God who is love. Having loved wholly he becomes love, and in the Eucharist we meet, not any effect or reflection of Christ, but his own person, given to us and universally present in its unique and particular human nature. We enter communion with the one who is the fully human sacrament and incarnation of God.

To talk of the universal presence of God in creation is an attempt to emphasize his concrete reality in matter and spirit, to remind us that created reality is always incarnate and unlimited. But it can become an abstract way of talking. We cannot after all really imagine *all* creation. Yet, out of a primary experience of love, we do believe. We commit ourselves to the vision of reality this experience initiates. To believe without imagining is faith. It is faith that is the basis of every degree of the knowledge of God. The meaning of the reality of the Eucharist is only available to one who is in this condition of faith.

If it is the nature of God to be universal, it is the ordinary nature of man to be particular. We know this because we have to make choices (and our fundamental choice is the assent to the gift of our own being). God, however, does not have to select, as all options coexist in his realized present moment. Man, in our as yet unrealized finitude, expresses the divine universality through the particular, and the particular is the creation of choice. The mystery of the Eucharist is the human mystery of Jesus choosing the particular meal of the Passover, with its particular (but universally meaningful) symbols of bread and wine, to express the universality, the divinity, of his love for his human brothers and sisters.

So, in a profoundly moving way, the Eucharist is the

expression of the weakness of man, his finitude. Some *one* thing had to be chosen to express what was universal. This is itself a manifestation of the tragic nature of our finitude, but it is wonderfully appropriate when we see it as forming part of the larger mystery of which the Last Supper was an effective symbol. This larger mystery is the Cross; or rather the acceptance of the Cross as the particular point where the love of Christ and his consequent vulnerability would reach its apogee. The silence of the Cross stirs an essential question in the heart of every man and woman. How did the finitude and weakness of the man Jesus break through to universal presence and power?

Limited and vulnerable Jesus was, like us. But he made what man alone cannot make – a complete and integral gift of self. His love for man was inherent in his fidelity to truth and this was his commitment of self to others. This is what makes him still the *man for others*. The completeness of this commitment was, of course, the love of God for man working in Jesus. It was not that he merely co-operated with this love, but he was one with it and was so in the beginning. True man and true God.

The folly of the Cross is the wisdom of God. Entire and unlimited as was the spirit of Jesus in accepting the Cross, it was still necessary that the Cross was an experience of final failure, defeat and death. But in the radiance of his integrity, the finality of the Cross becomes transformed into something of eternal meaning. It shows, to those who see it with faith, that the integral spirit not only survives death but is glorified, realized through death. The Cross is the extreme point of the development of human finitude, of man's being limited by the particular. But by the completeness, the wholeness of Jesus' commitment to this particular, it becomes the *universal* means of man's liberation into the reality of God.

In the Eucharist we encounter the frailty of the human, the immediacy and the ordinariness of the bread and wine and of the fallible, fickle human beings who constitute the community which itself is a vital part of the sacrament. We ourselves, as St Augustine said, are upon the paten that the priest raises to the Father. We also encounter the Cross. We die with Christ. But we do so in the power of the Resurrection which sheds its light both backwards upon the Cross and forwards upon the gathering together of all creation in Christ. The Cross remains a particular moment of complete human weakness. The Resurrection does not negate the tragedy of the Cross. But, like all moments, it is charged with the Presence, the power of God, realized in the Resurrection.

As the Mass transforms the ordinary into the mysterious (without betraying its particularity or frailty), so our meditation leads us from the particular to the universal (without betraying our wholeness or the strange gift of our mortality). No part of our life is left untransformed by meditation, because we meditate from the centre outwards and, as we travel deeper into this centre, the outward is transformed and unified with the inward mystery of God's presence. The mantra thus consecrates our whole life and, like the sacramental mystery of the Eucharist, it becomes an outward sign of an inner reality whose full realization is known only in faith.

Around the eucharistic table there are no observers, only participants. If anyone is there to observe themselves or others, then their presence is not real. The Lord is still present to them – for 'if we are faithless he remains faithful for he cannot deny himself'. And the complete and unconditional fidelity of his being present to us exposes us to a power of love that must eventually impel us to turn our self-centred attention outwards to him who dwells in silence and love within us.

This is the dynamic power of our stillness in meditation.. The part of our consciousness that is looking for results, searching for experience or calculating spiritual progress is simply not part of this movement towards God. That this part of us is of no significant power is a discovery we make on the pilgrimage. His Presence to us is stronger than our absence from him. All we need do is to enter the condition of faith that is our integral openness to his Presence. By our faithfulness to the mantra, our incarnate movement of faith, we thus allow the power of his indwelling Presence to radiate outwards, to be realized by our fully personal acceptance. Thus, we ourselves are made real by reality. Just as the Eucharistic community is made one by faith in the Body and Blood of Christ, so our personal inner unity is realized by the simple faith we bring to each of our particular times of meditation. And from that inner unity, we move outwards to realize our unity with others in the mystery of God.

Just as we see the presence of God in Creation because he is present within us, so we see reality because we are made real. And we are made real by his presence. The wholeness of God is such that it is only necessary to *be* in his presence in order to be transformed. It is vital that we learn to *be*. To learn it, most of us have to accept the ascesis of unlearning a great deal, both about God and ourselves. We have so complicated the simple truth we learn in meditation – that it is the wholly natural movement of our spirit to rise above all self-centredness by opening our consciousness to God *in the mind of Christ*.

The impersonal and materialistic assumptions our society creates in our attitude to life have done great harm to our understanding of the reality of prayer and to our capacity to pray. Above all they have replaced the value of *presence* with the idea of *function* – it is not what a person is but what he does that counts. The truth is that the value of action consists in the quality of being. Our experience of love is always contradicting the false assumptions, but they remain deep-rooted attitudes of the modern consciousness. Meditation challenges it at root, because when we meditate we are not trying to do anything: we are simply attending to the reality of the divine Presence and learning to be in that Presence.

We learn a little each step we take, each time we meditate, every morning and evening. More deeply we discover that to *be* is not to be isolated, but to be realized *in communion*. The Presence of Christ is eternally present to us and we grow in our capacity to be present to him. In that realization of mutual presence, of communion, the divine transcendence occurs and we are swept away from the netherworld of self-centredness into the infinite energy and complete fulfilment of the reality who is love. We send you encouragement and support in the commitment you are making to this journey into the reality of God. We keep you present in our heart and ask you to hold us in yours.

7

The Christian Crisis

In August Father Laurence conducted a retreat in Buffalo, New York, and another at Queen's University in Kingston, Ontario, in October. He also taught a course on the history and practice of meditation at Marianapolis College here in Montreal.

The first twelve of Father John's newsletters were published by Crossroads in New York under the title Letters from the Heart; Christian Monasticism and the Renewal of Community. *We were also preparing a pamphlet on conducting or starting a meditation group which contains a list of the groups around the world.*

Guests continued to arrive, enriching the community with a wealth of personal experience. Among them were the whole House of Bishops of the Anglican Church in Canada headed by Archbishop Ted Scott, the Primate.

We received several new oblates, and meditation groups continued to flourish in New York, Toronto, Montreal, Vermont and England.

It seems to me that the basic challenge facing the Christian Church is also a most vitalizing opportunity. This is the challenge and chance we have of putting before our contemporaries what we might describe as the basic Christian experience.

That may seem obvious enough until we distinguish between the basic experience and the superficial experience. The redemptive liberating power of Christ is announced at the superficial level but it is communicated, shared and known at the basic level of our being. This does not mean that the superficial levels of life are unimportant: our essential life and work is inseparable from our spiritual journey. But the superficial quickly becomes trivial, an empty sign, unless it is continually springing out of the depths of our spirit, where our whole being is centred, renewed and daily refreshed. It is peculiarly easy for religious-minded people to live superficially, alienated from the depth of the reality which they claim to be experiencing and proclaiming. The awareness of the perennial need to be authentically in touch with the experience of that depth is one of the essential insights of the teaching of Jesus and of the whole Christian tradition. To be a disciple of this Master means to be constantly mindful of the depth that lies beyond the surface, of the spiritual power that lies beyond religious authority, of the living person who lies beyond all theology and philosophy.

It is instructive to see how essentially Christian this sense of depth is. Look at the Letter to the Hebrews and listen to how curiously modern it sounds. 'Let us then stop discussing the rudiments of Christianity. We ought not to be laying over again the foundations of faith in God . . . Let us advance towards maturity, and so we shall, if God permits' (6:1,3). One can be quite sincere living off the ideas and images of our faith but, as our ordinary experience is constantly reminding us, sincerity alone is not ultimately satisfying. Our call as Christians is a call beyond thought and image and sincerity to that essential encounter with Reality, the encounter with Reality itself, and it is this encounter which makes us authentic. We are not only called, but are empowered to respond, because of the unique and fundamental transformation of our consciousness that has occurred as a result of the life of Jesus. The consciousness of a fully human being has opened in love to the infinite mystery of God. It has been swept out of itself into God but without ceasing to be itself. The mystery of the Incarnation means that Jesus remains fully human, fully alive to us and to the Father in his glorified state. And so it is through his human consciousness that we can make that same journey into authenticity: our call is to be realized by being bathed in the light of that reality, the reality that has glorified him. This is not only possible; it is, in a personal way for each of us, unavoidable – or avoided only at the cost of a wasted life. What the Letter to the Hebrews calls maturity, what St John calls 'the fullness of life', St Peter 'our sharing in the very being of God', St Paul 'the strength and power of his spirit in your inner being': all this is what modern man is desperately seeking. He is seeking to be made 'real'.

The Present Christ

There is a general sense in our society, I think, of the loss of power. The energy crisis we're all so familiar with is really a superficial expression of this deeper-rooted sense of the loss of spiritual power. Both physically and spiritually there is more than an element of absurdity in the 'crisis'. We talk of the energy crisis while at the same time we are the most wasteful and mindlessly over-productive generation ever to walk the earth. And we talk of the loss of spiritual power while we are, each of us, despite the powers of depersonalization that affect us, a temple of the living Spirit. Yet, the prevailing awareness of our time which underlies our experience and our fear of chaos is that our sources of power are running down. Not far below the surface of our frenetic activity and endless distractions is the fear that this is just as true of the spiritual and moral spheres as it is of the physical and social and economic spheres.

Of course there is a deep and complex interdependence between these areas. The visible surface of our lives is even more than a reflection of the state of things in the depths. It is part of the depths in the sense that our whole identity is the integration of everything we are. Moral choices are not the only criterion of our godliness but they are a vital expression of our oneness with the power that motivates a truly Christian morality – the power of love. That is why a Christian vision is one that sees surface and depths in the way that they do really correspond. Personal experience, as well as the larger condition of our society, should bear this out. It is little less than amazing that the social chaos that follows in the wake of economic crisis should so closely mirror the moral confusion that follows on the loss of spiritual power.

Our sense of an overriding crisis is realistic only if we foresee no chance of affecting the outward march of events through an interior change of direction. If, as the Christian vision claims, the external is intimately linked to the internal (surely this is what the Incarnation is about), a purification of our interior reality should result in the harmonization of external reality also. The social dream of the Gospel is one where charity, not exploitation, marks the relationships between people, where generosity rather than possessiveness controls the economy, where freedom not fear colours the psychological atmosphere. It is the dream, only partially and sporadically come true in

72

some Christian communities, of a revolution. But a Christian revolution is a revolution that must be energized by centrifugal forces – forces that radiate from the personal centre outwards. This is an ascending movement of liberation and expansion – not like most revolutions, a descending movement of aggression and constriction. The process that initiates this centrifugal revolution described in the Gospels is conversion, the interior, depth-turning change of the basic orientation of our being from self to beyond self.

Every conversion is a rediscovery of our true self and of our real participation in the Reality of God and is so much greater than our own limited potential reality. Every conversion – and, as St Benedict understood it, our whole Christian life is a conversion, a turning to God – is a further degree of awakening. The embedded momentum of our being urges us forwards towards full wakefulness.

> Awake, sleeper, rise from the dead
> And Christ will shine upon you. (Eph. 5:14)

To awaken is to open our eyes, and we open them, as St Benedict said, 'to the divinizing light'. What we see transforms what we are.

Each time we meditate we take a step further into this wakefulness, this state of being in light. And the more fully we integrate the basic Christian experience into our ordinary daily life the more deeply wakeful we become. This makes our life a journey of discovery, an exploration, a constantly renewed miracle of created vitality. To meditate is to put an end to dullness, to fear, and above all to pettiness. What is vital is that we are really on this journey, not just thinking about the journey or talking about it. A peculiar danger for religious people is to believe that because they are so religious they have all the answers taped. The frightful arrogance of the religious egoist is to believe that he has arrived before he has even started. It is easy to read about wakefulness, to have elaborate and, as far as they go, accurate ideas about enlightenment, and yet all the while to be fast asleep. The man who is awake knows without doubt he is awake. But the man who is dreaming also believes he is awake. In that state, the images of a dream convince us that they are the realities we know as real when we are awake. We enter wakefulness, as the meditator knows, by letting go of the images and by learning to wait for the Reality – for 'Christ to shine upon you'.

This is the basic Christian experience I was speaking of. It is perennial, unchanging, but also it is new in every generation and unique for every individual and unique every time we meditate. Every time we meditate we enter into the vitalizing creative presence of God. It is its manifold uniqueness that gives us our common ground, our oneness in him. This is the basis of all Christian community. The dynamic of the experience is always conversion, a turning from self to the Other, a rediscovery of a realm beyond ourselves and yet in which we have our own real and unique place. The dream image we let go of is of a universe revolving around us as its centre. The reality revealed – and the burden of illusion lifted – is the revelation that we are in our own unique and indispensable place in the universe, a universe that is centred in God, and which is permeated by his presence, for his centre is everywhere.

This rediscovery has a particular colouring in every time and place. Today the rediscovery we need is not primarily a religious one. We don't need, in the first place, to recover our identity in any superficial religious sense with any superficial religious demarcations – for example as good Baptists, Anglicans, Catholics or even Atheists. What we need is an experience of depth, to fill the surface with identity, with meaning, purpose and shape once again. This experience ensues when we make contact with our own inner spiritual nature, when we enter the structure of reality as it is established in our deepest centre, where the Spirit of God, God in all his fullness, dwells in love. Out of that contact – and the word is 'contact' much more than 'contemplation' – arises a deeply rooted and sane spiritual sense that will naturally communicate itself in the whole gamut of our religious, social, interpersonal and personal living responses to reality.

The call to modern man, the call to all of us, is to become spiritual, and to become spiritual we have to learn to leave behind our official religious selves – that is, to leave behind the Pharisee that lurks inside all of us – because, as Jesus has told us, we have to leave behind our whole self. All images of ourselves coming as they do out of the fevered brain of the ego, have to be renounced and transcended if we are to become one with ourselves, with God, with our brethren – that is, to become truly human, truly real, truly humble. Our images of God must similarly fall away. We must not be idol-worshippers. Curiously, what we find is that they fall away as our images of self fall away, which suggests what I suppose we always guessed anyway, that our images of God were really images of ourselves. In this wonderful process of coming into the full light of Reality, of falling away from illusion, a great silence emerges from the centre. We feel ourselves engulfed in the eternal silence of God. We are no longer talking to God or worse, talking to ourselves. We are learning to be – to be with God, to be in God.

That is why it is so important for all of us to learn to be still. In that stillness we learn to remain with the energy that arises from the contact we have made with our own spiritual nature. The phenomenon of so much contemporary 'spirituality' is not of a pilgrimage to the centre, but more like a raid mission that descends suddenly, plunders what can be got in the form of spiritual experience or insight, and then immediately retreats behind the walls of the religious ego. There is all the difference in the world – the difference between reality and illusion – between the pilgrim and the nomad. The pilgrim stays on the journey, steadily and selflessly, focused not on emotional or intellectual satisfaction but upon the goal, the goal that leads us, the goal who is Christ. This is true Christian conversion, the revolution that Christ taught and exemplified in his own person. It is what makes our beliefs credible – to ourselves and to others because it makes us credible. The steadiness – firmness, rootedness as St Paul described it – is the guarantee of our sanity. Our seriousness about the journey guarantees its joyfulness.

On the spiritual journey it takes more energy to be still than to run. I suppose most people spend so much of their waking hours rushing from one thing to another that they are afraid of stillness and of silence. A certain existential panic can overtake us when we first face the stillness, when we first enter into this state of pure being. But if we can once find the courage to face this silence, we enter into the peace that is beyond all understanding. No doubt it is easier to learn this in a balanced and stable society. In a turbulent and confused world there are so many more deceptive voices, so many calls for our attention.

But the Christian vision is uncompromising in its sanity, its rejection of extremism, in its invitation to each of us to have the courage to become ourselves and not merely to respond to some image of ourselves that is imposed upon us from outside. And the Christian vision proclaims to us that not only is this possible but the resources to achieve it are given to us, given to us in the power that is placed in our hearts as a result of the redemptive love of Jesus Christ. The Christian message is a message of limitless hope, because of the limitless generosity of Christ. But we would be foolish not to recognize that there is a certain austerity to the message too. Listen again to the Letter to the Hebrews: 'When men have once been enlightened, when they have had a taste of the heavenly gift . . . and after all this have fallen away, it is impossible to bring them again to repentance' (6:4, 6).

It is not that God withdraws his gift, as it were in pique; I think what the writer of the Letter to the Hebrews means is that, if we persist in treating ourselves trivially, we can mortally damage our capacity to receive the divine gift. The call to meditate every day of our lives is simply the call to take the words of Jesus seriously. We take them seriously by turning to his presence in our hearts every morning and every evening of our lives as our first responsibility.

We trivialize ourselves if we set limits to the energy available to us for this inner journey – the journey to our own heart, to the presence of Christ within us, and the journey beyond with Christ to the Father. The power source from which we draw our dynamism for this journey is inexhaustible, as St Paul tells us, 'It can be measured by nothing less than the power that God exercised in raising Jesus from the dead.' This power was exercised in the root of Christ's being, and Christ's presence is to be found in the root of our human being. The transformation that this exercise of the power of God brought about – 'the glory of the Resurrection' – was effected in the depth of the being of humanity as a whole. What each of us must realize is that in the depth of our soul we have died and we have been raised to new life in Christ. The basic challenge of our existence is to be open to the life of Christ. To be open to this life we must become fully alive. Only life can respond to life. Only in the loving attention of our own deep openness to Christ can we recognize that this life is the energy of the whole of creation, the energy of the Creator, the energy of love.

We can describe the journey as a journey from self-consciousness (the prismatic distraction and narrowness of the ego) to self-awareness (the clarified and expansive knowledge of our participation in reality). The Church itself is called to be a special sign of this transformation of consciousness. It is called beyond concern for its own image, its own success or its own influence. The Church is only itself when it is aware that it is the conscious presence of Christ in this world. This consciousness is the basis of its transcendent nature that can never be wholly institutionalized. The Church has always been vitalized and always will be vitalized by men and women who have the courage to tread this austere way, the way beyond self into the consciousness of Christ. The tradition that preserves, nurtures and communicates this awareness of God in Christ is the tradition of the Spirit present in the Church, enlivening the Church. All this suggests to us the primacy of the Spirit over the letter. Letters can only build up into the living Word that the Church must utter in every generation if the energy of new life is set free to enliven the letter, and this new life must be set free in the depths of our hearts. As Christians, we must speak a living Word to our contemporaries. It must be a Word that is authoritative, not authoritarian, a Word that is not sectarian, but is truly catholic. We can only speak this Word when we are alive with the life of Christ. The Church as envisioned in the New Testament is primarily a community of vitalized and enlightened brethren, illumined and charged with a life beyond their own – a life arising from the power of the risen Christ. The writers of the New Testament everywhere call on the early Christians to be open to this power. We in our turn, carrying on a tradition greater than ourselves, must call on our contemporaries to enter the dynamism of the marriage between God and humanity in Christ. But we can only do so when we ourselves have undertaken the pilgrimage to this union by our own selfless commitment to the pilgrimage.

What each of us must learn in the experience of our meditation is that the power for the pilgrimage is in fact inexhaustibly present. It takes only one step of faith for us to know that from our own experience. The important thing to remember is that one faltering but actual step is more valuable than any number of journeys performed in the imagination. As beginners we have to accept a certain distance between what we say externally, what we seek externally – and what we are internally. As we begin to tread the path that unites surface and depth, we have to recognize that we are limited, that we are sinners. What all this means is that we must understand that although we are setting out, we are only setting out, we have not yet arrived. Nothing is more likely to make us arrogant than to imagine that we have arrived before we have actually left. Leave we must. When we reflect on the necessity of this commitment it illumines the real opportunity and responsibility we have. Christ is consciously present in time only to the degree that we, his sons and daughters, open our minds and hearts to him in this world, only to the degree that we have undertaken the commitment to be real, to be still, to persist in reality. When we do embrace this commitment, the Church becomes in the first place not an institution, not an organization, not a hierarchy but the Body of Christ, filled in its every limb with his vital and vitalizing power. Not only filled with his power but – in the way of all conscious life – alive to that life in full self-awareness.

All this remains potential energy – not the kinetic energy which the Resurrection is – until we find the way to realize it. Commitment to the reality of Christ is in effect commitment to prayer. Prayer is our empathy with the consciousness of Christ, and in that empathy we know that his consciousness is of his infinite love for the Father, and of the Father's infinite love for him. Man's openness to this consciousness (the Spirit praying within us) sweeps us out of ourselves beyond ourselves into that stream of power flowing from the human heart and mind of Christ to the Father – to his Father – to our Father. Implanted in our human depths this stream is within time. So we return to our times of meditation each day, lest within the cares and concerns of time we forget the Supreme Reality in which we have our being, in which our being is rooted. As we do so faithfully and simply, as we follow the pilgrimage, we discover that the stream will carry us beyond time, beyond all division, and beyond all limitation into the now – into the infinite liberty of God. Unless we know the ordinariness of the way of prayer we fail to know the sublimity of its goal. Never forget the importance of the daily return each morning and each evening.

The essence of the Christian message is knowing this love and this power – although, as St Paul says, 'It is beyond knowledge.' So we must know it with a knowledge greater than our own knowledge because it is beyond the capacity of mere human knowledge. We must know this with the consciousness of Christ himself. This is the basic redemptive Christian experience.

The invitation we have is to be open, available to this experience. There are two elements to this. First, we must hear the Word of the Gospel, and this is not perhaps as easy as it sounds. There are many competing voices clamouring for our attention – most of them encouraged by our own egotistical spirit. But the Word of the Gospel is a call to sanity and, as such, it remains steady and strong in its utterance. The second step, once we have become silent and steady, and enough ourselves to hear it, is to 'remain within the Revelation'.

For all this we need the full resources of our humanity balanced and integrated. We need the strength and encouragement of the love of others in their humanity. But our deepest need is for the inexhaustible power of the love of Christ, the love of his human consciousness pervaded by the Light of the Father. The miracle of Christianity is that this need is already met. This power dwells within us, so far exceeding our need that contact with it sweeps us out of ourselves beyond anything we could have imagined or desired, into the reality that is the Kingdom. In the first step we take towards this power, his Kingdom begins to overtake us, to come to birth within us.

8

Self-will and Divine Will

New Year 1982 started with the simple profession of Paul Geraghty, who became the first monk professed for our Community, a sign for us all of our ever-deepening commitment into the heart of the Trinitarian Mystery.

As part of his ongoing commitment to the work of Christian unity, Bishop Henry Hill was appointed as the delegate of the Archbishop of Canterbury to visit Churches in the Middle East.

At the ceremony of Brother Paul's Profession, I spoke on the Benedictine vision of life. It is a vision that aims to make life more vital because, for St Benedict, the principal quality needed in a truly Christian life is an ongoing spirit of conversion. When this spirit is present in any life, there follows a continuous turning beyond the limitations of our own isolated and isolating self-will towards the divine will.

If our motivating force is self-will, we live in the prison of our own desires and disappointments. If, on the other hand, we have turned away from this force and are motivated by the divine will, we are swept into a liberty without frontiers in which everything in our experience is transformed into gift with epiphanies.

But those of us trained in a traditional religious vocabulary need to remind ourselves of the infinite liberty that is implied by a phrase like 'the divine will'. It is easy to limit this will by analogy to our own wants and needs and desires. The next step, following logically, but leading into absurdity, is to see the function of prayer as somehow influencing the divine will, trying to make the divine will coincide with our will. It is a good example of how dangerous and illusory any deduction or action becomes, whether in the spiritual or material sphere, when our point of departure is egoism. The actual experience of our potential for egolessness – our meditation – is, therefore, vital for a right ordering of our perspectives on reality. It is only when we begin the journey away from egoism that we can construct a religious language that really does make sense. From the basis of spiritual knowledge we know that to speak of the divine will is not to speak of what God wants – it is to speak of what he is. Then we will know, too, what Dante meant in his great saying, 'In his will is our peace.' What is the divine will? It is, simply, love.

Because St Benedict knew this mystery and lived out of it, his Rule can only be understood if we see the harmonious interdependence that he saw between obedience and love. In his vision monastic obedience was not mature while there was any trace of fear in it. We obey because we listen and respond out of love. This central and centralizing vision serves to align the whole person – body, spirit, mind and heart on the divine reality.

The actual experience of love, not the word, the theological idea or the dream, takes the life of the monk far beyond merely intellectual assent to certain propositions, even further from being a retreat from reality and it makes it instead into a life commitment towards truth, integrity and wholeness. Each of these ideals are deeply and humanly interwoven in the monk's daily life of prayer and work. Because of their fusion, their centredness in his own actual experience, he enjoys what is, perhaps, the essential gift of the monastic vocation – liberty of spirit grounded in wholeness of vision. He is able to commit himself to truth because the experience of love, welling up from within and so simultaneously greeting him from without, teaches him that this is the actual structure of reality. 'Happy are the poor in spirit.' This is the joy the monk knows in seeing how wonderfully simple all is.

Truth, integrity, wholeness. The ancient writers called these 'oneness'. If we fear the power of oneness, the experience of oneness, it is with good cause. It is the power of the living God which no dividedness or disharmony can withstand – and we are, all of us, absurdly attached to our own disunity and alien- ation. The detachment of the monk is essentially the renunci- ation of this absurdity which underlies all sin and the sadness and isolation consequent upon it. To pursue this new commit- ment to the reality of unity, to sense and sanity, requires courage, perhaps indeed a certain passion and recklessness. It requires the strength and flexibility of real humility, the capacity to learn about oneself, to find oneself and the gentleness and rootedness of true faith, the capacity to persevere in commitment to our gentle but uncompromising Lord.

The monk (*monos*) is, therefore, one who is one. One with himself because he can face and pass beyond all interior divisions. One with the brethren, not seeking his own convenience, but constantly turning to the community will, and one with God; the monk only fully becomes himself when lost in this oneness.

Benedict's understanding of conversion is of major importance, not just for monks, but for all who would try to lead a vital, which is to say, expanding Christian life. Our own practice of daily meditation is the essential expression of our commitment to the dynamic of conversion that unites our whole person, our complete life. It is impossible to convey this in words to someone who has not begun to experience it or at least to become aware of the possibility of it through meditation. It is one of the most inexplicable and frustrating limitations of the human condition, that the meaning of spiritual experience cannot adequately be verbalized beyond the community that the experience creates among those following the same path, regardless of who they are or where they are coming from. Of course, the attempt to communicate it is demanded of all in that community and the attempt more effectively succeeds when we realize that the experience is itself self-communication. Such is the Divine nature, which is love.

The self-communication of this redemptive experience progresses as we ourselves are unified by it. To be unified is 'to possess eternal life', as the New Testament puts it. This means that no part of ourselves, no aspect of our total human sensitivity is lost or destroyed.

One of the earliest things we discover when we begin to meditate on a daily basis, is that the practice itself begins to have results throughout our life. The harmonic sounded within us at the time of our meditation sets up sympathetic responses in every aspect of our personality and life. If it were not so – if our meditation were isolated in a spiritual vacuum – then we could be sure that the practice itself was illusory.

It is good to remind ourselves occasionally that meditation is not just another activity or interest in our life. It is so absolutely fundamental or central that we could say that it is, in a real sense, *lifegiving*. All life involves movement, growth, development. A person or an institution begins to die when their commitment to growth begins to wane. This is why our faith is, in effect, the energy that fuels the journey of meditation and, because it is a journey into God, our commitment is to a deep, divine principle of infinite growth. Our journey, like the Gospel itself, as St Paul describes it, begins in faith and ends in faith. Our daily commitment to meditation is the expression and renewal of our faith.

Conversion is to the spiritual life what revolution is to the political life. It is the free, conscious principle that assures freshness, honesty, creativity, all that we mean by integrity. As we all know, the ideal revolution is peaceful. It occurs in a society that recognizes the necessity for change as an indispensable part of the life and growth principle. It understands, also, that all the contributing parts of society, the groups or institutions, which are like the limbs of a body, stand in need of development if they are to meet new situations, new technologies, the new aspirations of man in the face of his own new discoveries. The creative energy activated in one part challenges the response of the whole.

The whole can only respond to the new situation created by an eruption of creativity, a new phase of growth, if it has already some genuine achievement of integrity. If, that is, it has a conscious centre. Unconscious centres are more common, of course – political powers or human hearts that operate by repression, out of fear, rather than by liberation, out of love. But the truly conscious heart – whether the centre of an individual person or of society – can cope with the new energies of growth, because it has already, up to that moment, to some degree harmonized the different forces that make up any organization. The centre is the open space where the paradoxes of being are held in dynamic and wonder-filled suspension. This dynamic suspension of conflict is both the goal of all life-oriented movement and the condition that makes growth, infinite growth, a realistic possibility. Another name for this dynamic suspension of paradox is peace.

The best revolutions are peacefully embraced. An orderly constitutional process of assimilation and advance is created and set in motion out of the great resources of power contained in the peaceful heart. The whole body politic is galvanized by this power. The more conservative and the more progressive forces unite maturely in a creative reassessment of the needs of society. An expansion of the circumferences is demanded by all in concert because the centre has produced more than the whole can absorb.

True revolution is motivated by this deep instinct to maintain, by expansion, the equilibrium between the centre and the circumference, between the parts and the whole. It is motivated, therefore, by a passion for peace. We have not really experienced peace if we think of it as the cessation or absence of violence. It is really the harmony of all the mighty forces that, disunited, lead to violence. Peace is not so much a consolation or an escape as a power in its own right and a rooting principle of reality. Like the word love, we use it loosely and vulgarly.

The social and political influence exerted by single individuals in history, men like Gandhi or Martin Luther King, an influence out of all proportion to their material power, should remind us exactly what it was that Jesus bequeathed us when he breathed on his disciples and spoke the word 'Shalom', peace, over them. Peace is an aspect of the human experience, of the human perception of the infinitely varied mystery of the will, the life, the love of God. It is a form of his energy which, like all energies, take their being from him. As such, it cannot be destroyed but is capable of infinite transformations. The Holy Spirit, which is the universality of God's power, his freedom to take all forms and his freedom from all forms, is therefore, for us, at the same time the love we find welling up in our own inmost heart and the power that impels us to realize equity and peace in our own societies. It is the power of all true peaceful revolution.

In the spiritual life, the same sort of principles apply. We do not approach true conversion of life with any sort of dramatic histrionics. We need the orderly, daily return to that process whereby we alter our angle of vision and so become capable of seeing the basis of all sovereignty. Because we are in a state of continuous conversion, we have never turned fully enough towards God. Each phase of growth clarifies and sharpens our vision further.

Self-will and Divine Will

Sometimes it is said that conversion is the spiritual law by which we learn to live by the will of God rather than by our own will. In a certain sense this is true enough. But what I think the practice of daily meditation soon reveals to us is that true conversion is much more a matter of learning to love as God loves.

St Paul tells us that there is a light shining in our hearts. St John tells us that this light is the point of divine consciousness, of infinitely pure love, to be found and worshipped in every person – the light that enlightens everyone who comes into this world. This is what it means to be human: to enshrine this unique and universal divine one-pointedness. St Paul and St John are, therefore, precious witnesses, but our own experience must then teach us that everything and everyone is enlightened by this same point that we find in ourselves – we must discover in a real sense that we are ourselves. We must become our real selves. The divine love is the originating and sustaining power of all creation and all consciousness. Our hopes for peace are not vain, because this experience of God, in the light of Christ that shines within us, brings us peace, unifies us, harmonizes our interior forces and satisfies our every desire, beyond the power of the imagination or heart to conceive.

Our life has to be a pursuit of wisdom because wisdom requires of us that we learn to live out of this light, this energy. To be wise is to be always in harmony with it and always vitalized by it. To slip out of this harmony, to descend from wisdom to mere cleverness is to begin to slide down the slope that ends in the hell of non-being. This slipping way is the reverse process of conversion. So, whenever a person is travelling in this reverse direction, he perhaps sees everything that a person in conversion sees, but does so in reverse, as mirror images of reality; whereas conversion leads us through love and life, its opposite creates non-love – the magician egoism, which leads through to non-being. Love is always creative; non-love is death-dealing. Conversion is commitment to the creativity of love. But to be turned towards non-love, egoism, is to be enthralled by the fascination for death. We find this in individuals as well as in societies. In both cases, material prosperity or production is no yardstick of true creativity. The only trustworthy measure is the depth of peace flowing from the centre that harmonizes all its parts in love.

Conversion requires in all of us significant readjustments in our life, in our angle of vision. These readjustments can be thought of but they cannot be effected by the power of thought. They can only be integrated into our life from the creative power that we find in our centre. That is why we best understand meditation, not as a process of self-improvement, nor as a tool we employ for desired ends, but rather as a process of learning, a process of wonder and deepening humility. We learn, above all, that God is the centre, the universal centre and the source of all that is. Everything begins in him and everything returns to him.

This, of course, is obvious enough but it becomes more challenging when we examine our own practice. The light which enables us to do this is provided by our meditation – here, as always, the touchstone is the degree to which we are living out the consequences of our meditation. How then do we live our lives, in fact? How do we arrive at our daily decisions?

Isn't it often the case that, in practice, the centre we align ourselves upon is ourselves? Seeing ourselves as the centre of the universe, we take our decisions, more or less, solely on the basis of how they will advance our own comfort, amusement or self-fulfilment. This self-centredness is our isolation – more terrible than any physical solitary confinement cell in the worst prison.

But, as we begin to break through our own egoism, we find that we certainly have a point of centredness, a place of our own but not the central place. Our destiny is to find our own insertion point in the cosmic reality of God's love. Only then can we love as he loves because only then can we be who we are. The power to love is only present in those who know or have begun to know who they are. This self-knowledge is not our own achievement or creation. It is potential for full being, created in the creative movement of God's love for us. We have being and we are persons capable of loving – which is to say, living the divine life, sharing the divine nature – because we are loved. This first step in conversion is, therefore, not renunciation, asceticism or any kind of suffering. It is allowing ourselves to be loved. If so many people never really begin the journey, it is because they have never drawn the curtains of their spirit and allowed the light of love to illumine their darkened hearts. There would be no greater tragedy than to die with such a curtained, untouched heart.

Once we are stabilized in our insertion point, we can come to the truth that sets us free, propelling us always further into the infinite liberty of God. It is the truth about him, the truth about ourselves and the truth of all that is. We can only see this truth with clarity of vision and in its totality if we are rooted and grounded in him. Otherwise, we see only aspects of things, unrelated to their convergent centre. So, in this fractured vision, we can never make valid judgements about the ultimate significance of the parts we see. Jesus has told us he is the truth; he is also the way because in him our vision is healed and focused. Through his life we can find our way into the place destined for us by his love.

Meditation is of such importance because we can only come to the truth if we have the confidence to face it. This confidence arises from the encounter with pure love in our own hearts. The really important thing to know in life – for life – is that he is and that he is love. It may be of some preparatory use to know also that we are sinners. But it is much more necessary to know and to know clearly, truthfully, that our sins are of no account. They cannot even exist in the light of his love, because they are entirely blotted out, burned away by that pure light.

It is very simple. The most important task of any life that would respond fully to its potential is that we come into this light to be purified, to be made real, to discover our own divine potential. The term 'enlightenment' is used widely today, and for those of us who follow in the footsteps of Christ, it is an important term. We can only see with his light. What we see transforms who we are. We become, as St John tells us 'like him'.

Perhaps the most valuable first lesson to learn is that the coming of Jesus, which we celebrated at Christmas, has transformed the ordinary. If we can see this clearly, we can see our own spiritual journey, our own religious practice, our personal life, all shot through with the transforming potentiality of Christ's redemptive love. In order to see this clearly, we have to understand how ordinary meditation is. Just as breathing is necessary for bodily life, so meditation is necessary for the development and sustenance of our spiritual life. To say the mantra is a very ordinary thing. It is of the same order as eating, breathing, sleeping. It remains esoteric only to those who have not yet undertaken the journey. To those who have begun, it is as ordinary and as wonderful as daylight. Like the other functions necessary for a balanced and healthy life, it requires a regular, daily commitment. But it is unique among these functions. It is the great integrating function wherein all our other processes are held in balance and aligned on the centre. Achieving, or realizing, the balance is the first step. From there on, we progress steadily into the heart of the divine Mystery.

The Church has a vital role to play in the world in calling people to this divinizing work. As far as I can see, very many of our non-religious, those we call secular, contemporaries are longing to hear this good news but we can only speak the enlightening word to them if we ourselves are on the Way. The Church has an unparalleled spiritual opportunity in this time, but it can rise to it only if we can find enough Christians to take Christ at his Word: 'Anyone who wishes to be a follower of mine must leave self behind' (Mark 8:34).

The faithful saying of our mantra is our response to this call of Jesus. It is work – the work of God. Above all, meditation is an all-out onslaught on egoism, on isolation and on sadness. It is an affirmation of consciousness and life through the experience of love. The Christian vision demands a community that is created and vitalized in the mind of Christ. The message this community must communicate is that it is possible for all of us to become alive with the life of Christ. It is not only possible, it is the destiny of each one of us.

The way to this vitalizing Christianity – a Christianity which is a light for the nations, the salt of the world and a power for peace – is the way of prayer: the prayer that is not our prayer but is the prayer of Jesus himself. That prayer is, even now as you read this, flowing in our hearts. Our meditation is our full acceptance of this ontological reality – the full acceptance of the gift of our own being and of the Being of God, fully embodied in Jesus. Our prayer in this vision is our life force.

9

A Way of Vision

Father Laurence returned from a six-week visit during January and February to Tanzania, where he gave a series of retreats and workshops on meditation. He was greatly gladdened by the many positive responses among both the African people and European missionaries. On his way back he visited Germany, where he conducted a seminar on contemplative prayer at the University of Würzburg, organized by the oblates there.

During the early part of 1982 several groups visited the monastery, ranging from the Knights of Colombus to a group from the Church of the Advent. A long-term guest, Dom Michael Hall from St Anselm's in Washington, D.C., participated in an ecumenical Lenten evening in St Bruno. We were also delighted to receive a visit from Father George Maloney, author of several books on prayer. We continued to receive new oblates in Toronto and Montreal.

Rose Lovat, our first oblate, was with us in March. She and Sister Madeleine Simon organized a meeting of the groups in London. From that meeting Father John went to Liverpool and Manchester to address the groups there and then on to Dublin to give a talk.

Easter was a full and joyful time for all of us here, and a time when we united to reflect upon the deepest mysteries of our life. We celebrate Easter liturgically over a few days but we discover its meaning only in a lifetime. Each year I hear these words of St Paul read out during the ceremonies and their significance seems to become both sharper and more real, urgent and yet more mysterious, each year. 'By baptism we were buried with him, and lay dead, in order that, as Christ was raised from the dead in the splendour of the Father, so also we might set our feet upon the new path of life' (Rom. 6:4).

To know this is to be a Christian, not just a member of a church or sect but a joyful personal disciple. It is to know that this new path of life is already opened up for us because of the energies set free among all humanity by the Resurrection. From our point of view we may see only the same tired, worn, old paths but if this Resurrection energy has touched us, if we have touched it in our hearts, the new path of life stands out brilliant and dominant, transcending all the old ways. As the snows of winter melted in our garden here a carpet of brown and withered leaves from last fall was exposed. As we started to rake them away we found that the earth was covered with young green shoots pushing up from the earth with an irrepressible energy – the energy of new life. We have to penetrate beyond the surface to make contact with the new life of the Resurrection.

The Resurrection is the eternal sign of our invitation to share in the glory, the complete realization of Christ. Just what does this new Resurrection-life mean? Does it have personal meaning for each of us or is it like a news item that everyone talks about and no one feels involved in? We find the answer, I think, in the New Testament accounts of the Resurrection. They all make it transparently clear that the risen Jesus could only be seen and recognized with the eyes of faith. 'She turned around and saw Jesus standing there, but did not recognize him . . . Jesus said, "Mary". She turned to him and said, "Rabbuni!" (which is Hebrew for "My Master") (John 20:14–16).

In the profoundly real and symbolic atmosphere of this encounter there is a marvellously condensed account of the human response to the Resurrection. We hear and see the Good News, but until the moment that it engages our absolute attention, by name, we fail to recognize it. When we do, all thought of self evaporates in the overwhelming joy of the reality so much greater than us, that can call us into itself. Mary is described as 'turning' twice, in this brief episode. For all of us there is this two-fold conversion that unfolds throughout a lifetime, the total conversion that demands absolute harmony of mind and heart.

Each of us needs this clarified vision that enables us to recognize what we see. Without this new dimension of faith we can only fail to see and to recognize the risen Christ within the creation he now pervades. Finding the power of vision which lets us see what is there, lets us see what is, requires of us the wisdom to penetrate the shell of reality, to go beyond appearances. This does not mean rejecting the ordinary or cultivating an esoteric 'essential' spirituality. Far from it. To go that route would be to remain locked at the most superficial of all levels of reality: the vanity of the self-centred consciousness, the egoism of the alienated 'me'. Penetrating the appearance of things means rediscovering in childlike wonder the divine and mysterious correspondence between appearance and meaning, between the mortal and the immortal. In the Christian vision of eternal life – which means full realization of all potentiality – nothing is rejected or wasted. Even our most fragile and ephemeral dimension, our body, is to be 'saved' from the entropic processes that so frighten us: so that as St Paul said, 'Our mortal part may be absorbed into life immortal' (2 Cor. 5:4).

We need the wisdom to search into the depths of things. We also need a deepening sensitivity to a dimension of reality which can only be revealed to those who want to see, who are humble enough to cry out with the blind beggar of the Gospel, 'Lord, that I may see.' (Mark 10:51). It is only the blindly arrogant who claim to see enough. Those who are beginning to see are aware of how much more their vision of faith needs to be purified. They know that no man can see God and live. The more we see him the further our self-consciousness contracts and our ego evaporates. To see God is to be absorbed into him. To have the 'eye' of our heart opened by the process of his love is to lose our very sense of the 'I' who sees. This is the sensitivity, the delicacy of spiritual refinement we need in order to see the risen Christ. It is the gentle delicacy that follows the cataclysm of death. It is the spirit of fully selfless love that does not flinch from being transformed into the beloved. 'What we shall be has not yet been disclosed, but we know that when it is disclosed we shall be like him, because we shall see him as he is' (1 John 3:2). There is an immortal power, the 'strength' of God, in this sensitivity. And that is why we cannot enter the new vision without finding a harmony with the basic structure of reality, without being sensitive to the truth that the underpinning reality of everything we see is God.

It is in this sense that meditation is rightly called a way of wisdom, a way of vision. Wisdom is more than the knowledge derived from accumulated experience. Vision is more than the power to visualize. To be wise we must learn to know with the heart. To see we must learn to see with the eyes of the heart – with love.

The only analogy I know of that does justice to this way of wisdom and vision is the analogy of falling in love. When we have fallen in love – and are still falling, still letting go of ourselves – the beloved changes before our eyes while remaining the same in all appearances to others not caught up into this vortex of love. Loving the other deeply and unreservedly, we see them in a new light which burns away (makes us forget) our own self-important isolation and allows the smallest gesture of theirs to reveal to us what no one else can recognize. That is why falling in love is so important for us because it sweeps us out of ourselves and beyond our limitations of fear and pride into the reality of the other. Until we can lose ourselves and find ourselves again in the other I don't believe any of us can ever know what liberty really is.

Profound meditation is of the same order. Our silence, stillness and our fidelity to the simplicity of the mantra serves to lead us away from our isolated self-centred view of life. We are only 'realized' or 'fulfilled' in meditation, because we have ceased to seek or desire realization or fulfilment. We only learn to be joyful, because we have learned not to possess nor to want to possess. The ordinary discipline of our daily meditation increasingly shifts our centre of consciousness from ourselves into the limitless Mystery of God's love. But first a certain effort is needed to root the discipline in our being rather than just into the routine of our day. We need to have it rooted as an interior as well as an external discipline, so that we can carry it with us through the inevitably changing circumstances of life. Even monasteries change their timetables! When the rhythm of the twice-daily meditation becomes part of the fabric of our being, entirely natural and so always renewed and renewing, then our life is being transformed from the centre outwards. Then we are learning to see even the appearances of our ordinary life, work, relationships with the vision of love. The Christian is called to see all reality with the eyes of Christ.

Because we are so used to remaining at the superficial levels of life rather than penetrating beyond appearances it can seem unbelievable to us that the way to real vision is the transcendence of all images. It seems to us, on the surface, that without images there is no vision, just as without thought there is no consciousness. What takes us this beyond this shallowness of unbelief? First, perhaps the frustration of shallowness itself, the frustration of finding that year after year we are penetrating no further into the real experience of life, into the real meaning of our own life. St Paul wrote, 'Your world was a world without hope.' This is the dilemma of the contemporary world. But what ultimately makes depth of vision possible is faith: the leap into the unknown, the commitment to the Reality we cannot see. 'What is faith?' the Letter to the Hebrews asked. 'Faith gives substance to our hopes, and makes us certain of realities we do not see' (Heb. 11:1).

The influence of the scientific method on our entire way of responding to life has persuaded us not to believe in, not to commit ourselves to, anything until we can see the proof of it. The method works well enough for the verification of scientific theory but it does not work in the dimension of reality that lies beyond appearances. There we must commit ourselves before we see God, because without that commitment there is no purity of heart, no undivided consciousness, and only the pure of heart can see God. The commitment must be unconditional, innocent of self-interest, childlike, 'a condition of complete simplicity demanding not less than everything'. It only requires a little experience of meditation to understand those words of Dame Julian.

Between the commitment – it can take us years to achieve it – and the vision there is a kind of hiatus. It is a vital interlude – what some men and women of prayer have called a glowing night – because it is here that we experience the loss of self which is the pre-requisite of the unified vision and wisdom to which we are summoned. The waiting is not a time of delay or postponement, as our instant culture would have us believe. It is much rather a time of joyful purification and preparation. It is a time of learning to be ready, ready to be disciplined, so that when the gift is given we will not try to possess it. It is a time of learning, that is, to say the mantra.

The saddest people that I have met in my life have been those who have in one way or another turned back from this vision, from the pursuit of this vision. It is, unfortunately, not enough to see the way or to understand what is demanded. Nor is it enough to become an expert in other people's experience. The only sufficient commitment is the total personal commitment of the childlike heart. As we begin to realize what is involved, all of us are tempted to compromise, to seek consolation in distraction, to turn back because we feel we haven't got what it takes to complete the journey to the other shore. That is why it is so important to remember the humility we need: the faith is the faith of Christ, the power to make the journey is given by him, if we can sufficiently acknowledge our poverty and so accept it.

The sign and the medium of this commitment is silence. By becoming genuinely silent, going beyond all images and thoughts, we quite naturally open the eyes of our heart to the light of infinity. We begin to see reality with a new power of vision, with a sharpness and acuity of vision which is startling and with a profundity which is intoxicating. What do we see? We see knowledge. That is, we see the One who knows that he is. We see oneness everywhere and at all times we know then with his knowledge that 'all must be one' – that is, all divisions must be transcended. We see love which is the supreme unifying power of creation. We see that all 'knowledge' and 'wisdom' are as nothing compared with the supreme all-inclusive Reality of the Love who Is.

When we set out we all imagine we will become wise or knowledgeable or at least that we will 'know' more. Gradually we become aware – a good sense of humour is essential for the journey – that this would be nothing but becoming more clever. At that point we must decide either for cleverness or for true knowledge. Rather than becoming more knowledgeable we become more loving, because everything is revealed to us in love. To see the world unified and to know ourselves as one, means that we are learning to love our neighbour as ourselves and to love God with our whole heart and whole soul. To love is to be *one with*. The infinite mystery of love, its intoxication and its boundless creativity is to discover the freedom that is given us when we love, and then the sheer wonder of discovery that we are loved in return. It is the Trinitarian mystery – Father, Son and Spirit – a mystery of reciprocal love.

We must be wholly committed. We must be ready. The revelation takes place in the moment of God's choosing: the co-mingling of the eternal with time. The Incarnation in each personal life is as it unfolds in its destined congruity with the one Incarnation, the one Resurrection. The only ultimate tragedy in life would be not to be ready for this moment of love, to be distracted at the time of revelation in which all time is transcended.

Our meditation and our daily recommitment to it is our setting out on the path of faith, which is the preparation of our heart for this moment. Day by day we leave all egoism behind and shed all divisions. We meditate in deepening silence in the humble acknowledgement that everything we can learn or experience is in the direct gift of God. Underpinning the journey and underpinning our deepening commitment is the simple acknowledgement that God is God, God is one, God is love. The moment of revelation is our entry into the eternal now of God. And so the revelation encapsulates, unifies all time. It unifies our whole life 'before' and 'after', just as the one Incarnation, the one Crucifixion, the one Resurrection embraces past and future in the eternal present. At this moment we recognize what we have been seeing. We know that we are called – by name, personally – into the ocean of oneness towards God. And we recognize the call because it comes from one of ourselves who has attained this oneness. It comes from our Brother, Jesus, our Lord, our Guide.

May his oneness, the power of his Resurrection inspire strength and guide our pilgrimage.

10

Parts of a Whole

We were delighted to be visited by the Abbot Primate of the Benedictine Confederation, who was visiting monasteries in North America. He spoke to us at Mass and we then introduced him to our many friends who have been such a support to us since we arrived in Montreal.

Bishop Henry Hill left us to visit Orthodox Churches in the Middle East and went on to Cairo. In June Father John had a most warm and encouraging visit with our groups in London, Liverpool and Manchester. In Ireland he went to see the sisters at Kylemore, and he then made a day of retreat with our Dublin groups at the Convent of the Sisters of Charity at Glenmaroon in Dublin.

Meeting and meditating with so many who follow the extraordinary and wonderful pilgrimage in the usual course of their ordinary daily lives makes me see more clearly than ever before the true nature of this journey we are making together. We know it as a journey of faith, of expanding capacity to love and to be loved; and so also as an expanding vision of reality. And we know it too as a way that demands more and more faith. Mountains get steeper the closer you approach the summit and the path narrows. But so also the view becomes vaster, more inspiring and more humbling, strengthening us for the deeper commitment required of us for the last stages of the climb.

We know too that our journey is a way of solitude. True, it is the end to loneliness and isolation. And the solitude becomes the real material of integrity which the love of God transforms into communion, into belonging and relatedness at every level of our lives. But still it is an ascesis, a continual purification, an on-going refining in the fire of love.

We best understand the true nature of solitude when we have

the opportunity of meditating regularly with a group. And what struck me so clearly in England and in Ireland is that this journey is a wholly personal journey. Each one of us bears the responsibility of responding to the call personally, committing ourselves personally. No one – neither parent, friend or church – can absolve us of this ultimate personal responsibility for accepting fully the gift of our own being and, by accepting it, for bringing it to its fruition in the mystery of its source and goal – the infinite love of God. But it is not, for all that, a journey we make alone. The Father of Lies, the ego, often makes his best converts among the most religious of us. Religious people are so prone to self-importance, self-fixation, self-dramatization. They can approach their spiritual progress or direction or vocation so self-centredly, so solemnly that the life of their religious response is stifled and becomes an inward-turning search for perfection, happiness or spiritual success.

The most vulnerable area of our spiritual journey in regard to the ego's ubiquitous assaults is that place where we choose between solitude and loneliness as the context of the journey. It is a real and crucial choice and one that has to be continuously reaffirmed by many of the decisions that life throws out, challenging us to self-transcendence, selfless love. So many – and it is the cause of the sadness and desperation of our age – choose to be lonely in the crowd rather than find communion in solitude. The community of the faithful, the monastery, the meditation group, the spiritual family, each one of these is the vital element in preparing us for this most important of decisions. Alone we can hardly see it, because when we are isolated we cannot see beyond ourselves: this is the terrible delusion of self-centredness. But in contact with others we awaken to the deeper truth of our being that we are meant to see, and so we learn to travel beyond ourselves. This is why meditating regularly, whether daily or weekly, with the same group or community is such a source of healthy sustenance to our pilgrimage. We cannot maintain the delusion of an isolated pilgrimage when we are present with others. And yet, this very physical and spiritual presence recalls us to a deeper personal commitment to stillness, to silence and to fidelity. The group or community similarly signals the end to all false heroism and self-dramatization. Being in touch with the ordinary failings and limitations of others puts our response and fidelity into the perspective which we need for balance and harmony in our life. In the presence of others we know ourselves.

The Christian life summons us to loss of self and we lose ourselves in the love we have for others. One of the Desert Fathers returned from his hermitage to the community speaking of the dangers of spiritual pride when separated from others, and then he added, 'There, when I was alone, whose feet could I wash?' The life of charity, of practical other-centredness is not only an experience of the experience of Christ. It is the great stabilizing and enriching element for all who would find a contemplative dimension to life. The great decisions that place us deeper in reality or thrust us further out into lonely illusion are not the decisions between extremes. They are the decisions that are the hardest to make for they are the ones that keep us on the path we are already treading, that make us more centred, deeper rooted. One of the fears people often feel as they go deeper is that their options are diminishing, the ways of escape are getting fewer. The narrowing of the road is a cause for joy because it is a sign we are approaching our goal. I was deeply moved and inspired by the groups I met with in England and Ireland. They showed me the importance of seeing the pilgrimage of meditation in terms of spiritual health and psychological balance rather than as something esoteric or precious. They showed me too how desperately our society needs men and women seriously committed to persevering on this Way to the Absolute. The ordinariness of the weekly meetings, the simplicity of their organization actually highlights the sublimity of the pilgrimage these people are following. They are truly leaving self behind and entering into the infinity of God's love.

A person does not start to meditate because he feels it will help society. Perhaps he even regards his meditation as his ration of personal self-concern over and above what he does in the rest of his life to benefit others. But after some experience of the nature of meditation and of the profound (though often silent and at first inconspicuous) change it makes in one's life, we all begin to see things differently. Our progress on the pilgrimage clarifies, through lived experience, what we mean by saying that 'being is prior to action' or that the significance and quality of what we do depends upon our capacity for simply *being*. This remains a philosophical proposition before we have begun to meditate, but (as with so many other ideas of our faith) contact with our own reality transforms static theory into the wonder of personal discovery. The more fully we open our eyes to the fundamental and all-pervasive mystery of being, the more clearly we see the true place and nature of all activity. The same clarifying process transforms our view of the pilgrimage as well.

We all begin the pilgrimage with a certain degree of egoism, self-centredness, seeing everything in its relation to ourselves. In effect, we see ourselves as the centre of the universe. This applies even to our meditation itself when we begin. But as we progress we lose this self-centred tendency of our perception and we become more other-centred in our understanding. We see that even our meditation itself can *only* be other-centred. That is, concerned not primarily with ourselves but the other who is, who was and who always will be with us: our brother, guide and Lord, the Christ whose centre is simultaneously in God and in us.

Somebody asked me at one of the meetings how meditation fitted in with the vision of the whole human race in its movement back to God through evolution and through free will. Is the Christian one of the elect, the tiny minority from among all races and generations who will awaken to God? And if so, does that mean that the Christian meditator is one on the inner track among the elect? It is an important question.

Every day I am more amazed at the range and variety of people who really *hear* the message of the teaching about meditation, who hear it from some deep and perhaps unsuspected stillness within themselves. And I am even more inspired that so many remain faithful to the discipline and the fidelity that makes the hearing really significant. They are people of all ages and backgrounds, educational, social and religious. But they have all discovered a common centre, Christ, who lives in their hearts and in the heart of all creation.

It would not be easy to generalize about what else they have in common. It is certainly nothing as superficial as an I.Q. rating or an interest in things religious. The wonder of the community of those on the pilgrimage is that it is really only their experience of faith that makes them seem the same. And the very wonder is that this faith is pure, unpredictable, invincible and pure gift. That much we know but according to what purpose or design the gift is given we are much less knowledgeable. The phenomenon of God's self-revelation and embodiment among mankind is the purest of mysteries, knowable but beyond understanding. To know it is to be made real and to be set at peace. To strive to understand it is to strive vainly to go beyond the limits of what is the specifically human reality.

Nevertheless, although this may seem to be pointing towards a spiritual elitism it actually reinforces the solidarity, the interdependence and equality of the whole human family. Precisely because our capacity to *hear* and to *respond*, the capacity we call faith, *is* pure inexplicable gift, it is no cause for pride. Because the source of the gift is God, it cannot be purely arbitrary or without meaning.

The meaning is this: by hearing and responding, by pursuing the call to poverty of spirit and purity of heart, we discover that within the depths of our being we fulfil our part of the divine plan for the whole of mankind. The mantra is, as experience proves, an act of pure love, universal love. Everyone who meditates faithfully through all the personal storms and challenges of their personal life begins to know this. They come also to know that they are meditating through the crises and tragedies of their world. Indeed the further they go on their way, the closer they realize they are to the Whole which is more than the sum of its parts. It is so because the Spirit moves among it, giving it that completion, that redemption which is the centre of God's design. The communion we discover in the solitude of our own hearing and responding is not only communion with ourselves. That is perhaps the first sign we have of it – a deeper personal harmony and freedom. But it persists beyond, to the communion we share with all men and women, with all the dead and all the living and the yet unborn. With them we share the great and mysterious gift of life in the flesh and in the Spirit. And as we awaken to this deeper and higher sense of wholeness we sense the ultimate all-embracing communion which contains all this and of which these are epiphanies. The communion we have with God and the communion within God – this is the great truth we encounter. All we can say in the end is what we said at the beginning – that the meaning of life is the mystery of love.

Because of our incorporation in the whole – an incorporation that has both material and spiritual dimensions – every experience in the human family influences the whole. This is why St Paul calls the early Christians 'to weep with those who weep and to rejoice with those who rejoice'. Violence, injustice, and all suffering anywhere within the Body of Christ affects and implicates us all. The reality is that we are not isolated. We are one with the One. We are one with all.

And yet we are more than component cells in a huge organism. We are each of us given a unique and essential place within the infinite mystery of God. We each of us have a personal call to *hear* and to *respond*, and if we fail then the whole is impoverished.

In breaking through the walls of egoism and fear that so often encase our hearts, the light makes that beam itself universal. The mystery of love is that we become what we delight to gaze upon, and so when we have opened our hearts to this light we become light. We still are ourselves, for God does not remove his gifts – they are given in his eternal present moment. But we are transfigured, burning with a light brighter than ourselves and however dark is the world we are in, this light cannot be extinguished.

To judge only by appearances, materialistic or institutional, one might be tempted to say that the Body of Christ is being broken down in our world. But it is in fact being built up! Often in very human, unexceptional incarnations which testify to a power beyond themselves, beyond appearances, beyond all materialistic notions of success. I felt this very strongly meeting with so many meditators in England and Ireland where individual fidelity and group witness were open doors for the transfigured light of Christ in homes, schools, factories, offices and hospitals. In all these places the human consciousness of Christ made its appearance in the human consciousness of those who seek him daily in all humility. In London and in Dublin where our groups had a whole day together many people came to me afterwards and said how extraordinarily happy and peaceful the day had been, and what a power of love they had felt flowing around them. We are, all of us, moving towards the love, and the light is moving towards us. But we are, none of us, trying to possess the light for ourselves. It is 'the' light rather than 'my' light. And there is only one enlightenment – the opening of the human consciousness of Jesus in that light because he is incorporate in our humanity. We are, all of us, affected by that enlightenment. Indeed his light is what we call our redemption. We are redeemed in the light of his love.

To try too exclusively to understand this might lead us to pride. To *know* it in the ordinary fidelity of our pilgrimage is to be rendered humble by the sheer wonder of it. We each of us have a unique and urgent responsibility to know it. Once we hear, we must respond as fully, as generously as we are called to. For when the light and the kingdom dawn in our hearts, it then touches all we touch. We must not fear the dawn, for the light must dawn and burst and expand in our hearts until it becomes the full dawn of the Resurrection.

11

Beyond Memory

The highlight of summer 1982 was a holiday we had together as a community in Nova Scotia. We stayed, through the generosity of the sisters of the Congregation of Notre Dame, in their house on Iona, a lonely island of the Bras d'Or Lakes.

During the summer and early autumn three new groups started in New York City and New Jersey. We received new oblates from Toronto, Los Angeles, Boston, Calgary and Montreal. At our last oblate meeting we were pleasantly surprised to discover that the oblates had organized a fifth anniversary party for us and had invited a large number of old and new friends.

Early in October Father John spoke to the Palliative Care International Conference at its meeting here in Montreal. There were a thousand or so participants whose work is to look after the terminally ill. It was a wonderful opportunity to speak to a large group of sensitive and caring people on the importance of meditation as the Way. It was at this time that Father John became aware of his own approaching death.

In talking to the Conference on the care of the dying I tried to show them that meditation is a way of growth and development. In a real sense it is the way of growth because what we are growing into through meditation is life itself. It makes us more full of life and therefore more fully alive. Although meditation obviously has some characteristics in common with our other experiences of growth and development (as, for example, the pain that accompanies all growth), it is different from these other experiences, which we usually perceive as growth into greater complexity. But meditation is growth into greater unity, into greater simplicity.

Unity is freedom. Whoever has realized his own essential oneness can easily pass into the reality of his unity with others.

And this realization of oneness is the *raison d'être* of all consciousness. Unless we are on the way to this realization our life lacks meaning and we live our life as if it were a battle against discontent rather than as a celebration of joy in the fact that we *are*. The only ultimate tragedy in our life would be never to realize any part of this oneness and to remain bound by our limitations. The only significant limitations in life are, therefore, those which retard our entry into full unity. In a materialistic view we regard as limitations whatever restricts our freedom of action – illness, poverty, misunderstandings beyond our control. Naturally these imperfections have to be combatted by our life-force and our innate love of goodness. But we can be ill, poor, misunderstood and still be free. We can suffer these forms of external limitation and still be joyful in the gift of our being. We can be restricted in our ability to move, even to communicate and yet still be in communion, *in unity*. The really dangerous limitations are those that arise not from our physical dimension but from our egoism, our preference for isolation, our self-centredness, the reification of self, others and God.

Meditation is a gentle way of growing into the freedom that is beyond all limitations of this dangerous kind. It is not magical. Meditation does restore us to a deeper harmony of body and spirit, but it always remains an essentially *spiritual* growth. All growth is a form of healing. Not just a retrospective healing of past wounds but it propels the whole person we are *now* into greater wholeness, the health we are created for. And so we can say that meditation is a growth beyond limitations that prevents us from being whole, entire, in 'divine health'.

Once we pass a limitation that has previously held us back we discover that we are free from it for all eternity. We are no longer dominated by the fear or the narrowness that limitations impose on us and which can seem, while we are in their power, to be immovable. Time is so precious for us because we must use the unique opportunity time gives us to grow as completely as we can beyond all limitations. Time used for liberation prepares us to enter into eternity as persons who are essentially free to *be* fully alive. What we call eternal life is the state of perfect oneness, and it demands that all those who enter this unity are personally free to do so – free to be, free of self-consciousness, free to love, free to commit ourselves without reserve.

The process of growth into freedom is an essential aspect of the divine dimension of human life and consciousness. God is the one who is infinite growth, infinite and perfect freedom. He is the one who is complete. As I have suggested before, divine perfection is not a static achievement. That is why it is not something that we can contemplate as a fixed object within horizons of our own making. God is quite other than the monumental image we so often picture him as being. He is Person. To be personally complete is simply to be free from all the limitations that restrict us from expansion, and God is precisely the infinite expansion who is perpetually centred in himself. And he is centred in every human consciousness through the unique human consciousness of Jesus. God is complete and he is completeness itself. That is why the state of completeness is always *present*. It is never future or past. God is always now. Our meditation is always concerned with another step into the present moment and it is growth to the degree that we allow ourselves to take this step unconditionally. It is always another step into the eternal *now* of God. Every time we meditate we take another step into the divine life that enlivens, brings to fullness, everyone who opens himself to it by taking this step of turning from self. The paradox we discover in the course of taking this step day by day arises from the divine paradox – a life which is wholly present, wholly without reverie or daydream, where everything is actualized and complete, and yet which is always expanding in self-transcendence. The divine paradox is love.

Like all growth, this entry into the divinizing experience of the present moment involves pain. It is the pain of all maturing. It arises from the need to leave behind us every earlier stage of development, all that we have been, in favour of what we are summoned to become. The transition from time to eternity, which is this growth, is continuous. Every moment is a dying to the past and a rising to a new present in which the past is not rejected – we are who we have become through the experiences of a lifetime – but in which the *memory* of the past is allowed to crumble back into the dust from which it was formed. No *memories* can survive the transition from incompleteness to fulfilment. In a sense the limitations we are talking about are all the limitations imposed and sustained by memory. We have to forget, to *unknow* everything we have been if we are to bring ourselves to completeness. Much of the difficulty involved in overcoming the limitations imposed by memory is that we have to learn to let go, of not just part of ourselves, but the whole of our self-consciousness. We can only become fully present to the now of the divine moment if we can leave the past behind totally.

What we try to do is to maintain observation points, base camps along every stage of our development. Each of these little camps is an outpost of the central H.Q. of the ego. Each of them becomes a link in the chain of command stretching down from the ego into every corner of our life as part of the ego's attempt to bring all life within its sway and to cast its net over our whole consciousness. At each of these observation points we are tempted to hang on to part of ourselves on the brink of the new stage of growth. But if we opt for this, then instead of our life becoming an experience of accumulative growth, we find our lives contracting. Instead of finding that there is more and more space of consciousness to fill by our accepting the gift of Being and love, we will find that the net of self-consciousness will tighten around us and persuade us there is less and less space to expand into. Our life becomes progress into a cul-de-sac rather than progress across a bridge to the further shore.

At each stage of growth we have to leave all of ourselves behind and go forward, becoming a new creation. Accepting this perspective as a workable theory of life, just believing in it, is not enough. We all know how dry and unsatisfying a state we are in when we have all the right theories (with all the possible variations on them duly categorized and discussed) and still have not found the *practice*. It was of this state that Jesus was speaking when he said that to those who have, more will be given, and to those who have not, even what they think they have will be taken away. It is a hard saying but one whose truth we can all recognize. What is perhaps harder to recognize is just where we are. *To have*, in this saying of Jesus, means to be a follower of the Way, our feet really touching the pilgrim path each step we make. *To have not* is to be buoyed up along the path by theories of the pilgrimage and so to be treading air, marking time and losing time. It is difficult to accept that

106

we may fall into the second category. Our theories can make us impotent and self-important, like people with a car manual but no car. We do not like to admit that we may not have been really making the pilgrimage up to this moment of truth. Yet the humility to accept this, to make a new beginning is demanded (and re-demanded) of us, if our feet are ever to touch the ground. If not, then what we think we have – our theories, which are too inadequate to express any but a part of the whole mystery at any one time – will be swept away from us when reality dawns. It does dawn for all of us, whether we are ready or not, when death removes the superstructure of limitations that we can so easily mistake for reality.

We need to pass through theory into actuality, and this is just what we do each time we meditate. Everything we have been and everything we have done up to that moment is abandoned when we sit down to meditate. The more fully the past is truly abandoned, the more completely renewed we are as we return to the work of our day. Meditation is a continuous breakthrough into the present moment of God. This is why we can begin to understand the mystery of this process of growth only if we see it in the perspective of our whole life. The person who meditates is the person we *are* – the person we become from birth to death – the whole person. Not the isolated image of self we usually identify ourselves with while we are moving in and out of one or other of the phases of our life.

Our growth in and through meditation is not, therefore, restricted to isolated experiences. That is why concern for what we are experiencing from day to day is so counter-productive. Spiritual growth is always growth into union which means growth out of self-consciousness. If we have this essential principle of reality made concrete in our daily fidelity to meditation we are in the happy position of one who enjoys the humble and yet absolute confidence of St Paul's Christian who, 'gifted with the Spirit, can judge the worth of everything'. Rooted in this actualized pilgrimage, we know whether anything advances or retards the growth towards completeness in Christ. Does it make us think more about ourselves or less about ourselves? That is the Christian touchstone.

Monitoring our experiences is an attempt to fix God in time and so to stifle his own expansion – the Spirit. And as soon as we do this, we experience not God but only our own egotistical image of God. Strictly speaking, meditation does not give us any 'experience of God'. *God* does not experience himself; rather, he knows. For him to experience himself would suggest a divided consciousness, a limitation to his own perfect freedom. The knowledge God has of himself is one with himself. His self-knowledge is love.

Meditation takes us into this self-knowledge which is the life of God. It is a life full of the knowledge of the self born from self-transcendence. This is why meditation is an entry into divinization through Jesus. Through our union with him we pass the limitations of division and become one with God. Through him we utterly transcend ourselves, leaving our whole self behind and becoming a new creation in him. Meditation is itself the process of self-transcendence. To the degree that we are transcending self we are divine because we are becoming one with the power of love.

Our spiritual growth can never be seen as an *accumulation* of experiences, rather it is the *transcendence* of all experiences. What we so often call a memorable experience is first and foremost a memory. But in the eternal act of creation which is the life of the Trinitarian God everything is *now*.

We must not become self-important about our self-transcendence. We can occupy the centre of our imaginary universe so completely that it seems to us the world would fall apart if we abdicated from our position at that centre. Of course, the only world that does fall apart is the mirror-image world of egoism. The real world comes into being for us as we ourselves become a new creation.

Small though the relative cosmic impact of our little self-transcendence may be, it has absolute value. The completion and the liberation of the human consciousness is after all the central meaning of the entire mystery of God's creation. So each of us, by our own little liberation, is empowered to become one with him. We must never forget this if we are to remain rooted in the expansion of the divine life, if we are to grow. Each time we sit down to meditate we enter into oneness – the oneness of God who is now, the oneness of God who is love.

We can't really understand this vocation to unity. It is too much for the mind to hold or imagine, except in fragments. But what we can do is to sit down and say our mantra. To do so with humility, fidelity and absolute trust in the goodness of God who calls us beyond every limitation to become like him. He calls us, such is the marvel of the Christian revelation, to expand into his infinity.

The more we contemplate the wonder of our vocation the more humble we must become, the more poor in spirit. We become humble and poor by our fidelity to our mantra. It sometimes seems to us at the beginning that as we make progress we won't have to say the mantra quite so faithfully in the future. But as we do progress, in actuality not in imagination, we discover that we must enter more and more completely into the poverty and fidelity to which the mantra leads us.

12

The Oceans of God

In the later months of 1982 we enjoyed visits from many guests from many places. A nun from Stanbrook Abbey enlivened the Community with her stories about monastic life on both sides of the Atlantic. Other guests included Burkard Schuhmann from Würzburg and Sister Camille Campbell, who has joined us for a year to help run the guest house.

Monastic Studies 13 *was published and received a very good welcome. We are happy that it has been possible to revive this excellent journal of monastic scholarship and to continue its high standards.*

We had a special weekend at the monastery during which artists, poets, sculptors and musicians who meditate with us shared their work and discussed the spiritual value of art. Having meditation as the common bond between all the participants seemed to assure a real foundation for the exchange that took place.

In London, Sister Madeleine Simon started a 'Christian Meditation Centre' from which she distributes the newsletters, runs several meditation groups and organizes a focal point for advice and resources for all the meditation groups in England.

A collection of the first twelve of these newsletters was published, under the title Letters from the Heart, *by Crossroads, New York, and distributed in England by the S.P.C.K. The introduction gives a history of the beginnings of the Montreal community with some thoughts on the emergence of a contemporary monasticism rooted in the tradition of 'pure prayer'.*

[Father John gave these news items in this his last newsletter; it gives his definitive teaching on a Christian's readiness for death.]

At Christmastime we become more sharply aware of the

mysterious blend of the ordinary and the sublime in the monastic life and indeed all life that is really Christian. It is important, though, to see it as a blend not as an opposition.

It is tempting to treat the birth of Christ as something romantically outside the full meaning of his life, something pre-Christian. In the rich and beautiful gospel accounts of his birth we can be tempted to see this part of his life as merely consoling or idyllic. But it is part of the human mystery that nothing is outside the Mystery. By the Incarnation God accepted this aspect of the human condition and so the birth and childhood of Christ are part of the mystery of his life – a life that culminated on the cross and reached its transcendent completion in the Resurrection and Ascension.

Our meditation teaches us how fully every part of us has to be involved in the radical conversion of our life. It teaches us that we have to put our whole heart into this work of the Spirit if we are genuinely to respond to the call to leave the shallows and enter into the deep, direct knowledge that marks a life lived in the mystery of God. Then everything in our life acquires this depth dimension of divine Presence. We are foolish to look for 'signs' on the way – it is a form of spiritual materialism that Jesus rebuked – because if we *are* on the way, which means in the Mystery, in the bright cloud of God's presence, then all things are signs. Everything mediates the love of God.

There is, of course, literary art in the infancy narratives of Luke and Matthew. But this does not mean that the details of the birth of Christ were not charged with wonder and mystery for those who were involved in it. The parents of Jesus 'wondered' at what was being said about him. And Mary teaches us how this experience of wonder is to be assimilated by 'treasuring these things in her heart'. The 'heart' is that focal point in our being where we can simply be in the Mystery without trying to explain or dissect it. A mystery analyzed becomes merely another problem. It must be apprehended whole and entire. And that is why we, who are called to apprehend it, must ourselves be made one in heart and mind.

The mystery surrounding Jesus was perceptible from the beginning of his life. Not until his death and resurrection was it capable of being fully apprehended, fully known. Because not until then was it complete. Our life does not achieve full unity until it transcends itself and all limitations by passing through death. This is why we do not fully comprehend the mystery of Christ, in which we enter the mystery of God, until our life is complete. We begin to enter it as soon as our consciousness begins to stir into vital perception and to learn the laws of reality by learning to love and be loved. But we are always learning, always preparing for the fullness that comes to us all. Until the life of Jesus passed through death and returned in the Resurrection this completion was a source of terror or despair to the human race. Now it has been transformed. For what seemed a dead-end has now been revealed to the eyes of faith as a bridge. This is the hidden significance of the birth of Jesus, his growth through infancy and manhood and his supreme sacrifice of self on the Cross. In our beginning is our end. And so in the birth of Jesus death already began to be transformed. All the intuitions shared by those involved in his birth and his early life were fulfilled in his ministry and the paschal mystery. His life, like every human life, has a hidden and mysterious unity. End and beginning are two ends of the string of life held in the mystery of God and joined together in the mystery of Christ.

Our life is a unity because it is centred in the mystery of God. But to know its unity we have to see beyond ourselves and with a perspective greater than we generally see with, when self-interest is our dominant concern. Only when we have begun to turn from self-interest and self-consciousness does this larger perspective begin to open.

Another way of saying that our vision expands is to say that we come to see beyond mere appearances, into the depth and significance of things. Not just the depth and significance in relation to ourselves is involved but depth in relation to the whole of which we are part. This is the way of true self-knowledge and it is why true self-knowledge is identical with true humility. Meditation opens up for us this precious form of knowledge, and it is what enables us to pass beyond mere objectivity – merely looking at the mystery of God as observers – and to enter the mystery itself. This knowledge becomes *wisdom* once we have entered the cloud of the mystery and when we know no longer by analysis and definition but by participation in the life and spirit of Christ.

So we learn by the path of meditation what cannot be learned otherwise, what is unknowable as long as we hesitate to become real pilgrims of the spirit. Following this path is a fundamental requirement of the Christian life which must be a life lived out of the depths rather than the shallows. This is why Christian discipleship is the completion of the human condition. In this condition man always seeks the *complete action*, something that will call forth all his powers simultaneously, focus and unify all the dimensions of his being. Until we have found this action we are restless, always mastered by distraction or desire masquerading as the reality which only this perfect action can lead us into.

Naturally, if we are truly human we know that this action is love. Only when we live in and out of love do we know that miraculous harmony and integration of our whole being which makes us fully human. This is always a practical rather than idyllic state: I mean that the human condition is always made up of frailties and imperfections, either of personality or environment. The Incarnation of God in the human condition, however, absorbs all these faults and accidents in such a way that they can no longer prevent us from the fullness of love. The saint is not super-human but fully human.

Every part of us, including our faults and failures, must be included in our commitment to the pilgrimage into this fullness. Nothing real is excluded from the kingdom of heaven. Realistic, human wholeness is the accumulative experience of staying on our pilgrimage. Gradually the separate compartments of our life coalesce. The room dividers are taken down and we find that our heart is not a prison made up of a thousand individual cells but a great chamber filled with the light of God whose walls are constantly being pushed back.

Meditation expands our *knowledge* of God because, in leading us into self-knowledge, it propels us beyond self-consciousness. We know God to the degree that we forget ourselves. This is the paradox and the risk of prayer. It is not enough to study the paradox because, like love, it can only be known when it is lived firsthand. Once we have begun to live it we can read the great human testimonies of the spirit – the New Testament and the spiritual classics – from within the same experience. Until then, however, we are merely observers, at best waiting to begin.

It is not an easy paradox to grasp. How *can* one grasp the spirit? It helps though if we reflect on the human manifestation of this essential structure of reality. To love another person involves more than thinking of them, more even than enjoying their company, more even than sacrificing oneself for them. It involves allowing ourselves to be loved by them. This is perhaps the most moving and awe-inspiring mystery of the Incarnation. In becoming human God allows himself to be loved within the human range of love, as ordinarily as any infant, child, adolescent or adult.

The humility of God in allowing himself to be loved in the man Jesus is our cue for recognizing the basic structure of all reality. Our first step in loving God is to allow ourselves to be loved. The grammar of language is misleading here because there is nothing passive about allowing ourselves to be loved. Just as there is nothing passive about turning our attention off ourselves and nothing passive about saying the mantra – which are the ways we allow ourselves to be loved in any human or divine relationship.

Meditation takes us into the basic relationship of our life. It does so because it leads us into the intimacy with God that arises out of the eternal reality of his loving and knowing us. In doing so he calls us into being and *human being* is itself a response to the demand inherent in God's love and knowledge of us. It is the demand that we love and know him. Yet, we can only know him, not as an object of our knowledge, but by participating in his own self-knowledge, his life, his spirit. Thus we are led back to the starting point of our being, his love and knowledge of us. We come to know and love God because we allow him to know and love us. We allow his self-knowledge to become our self-knowledge. This is the alchemy of love.

Knowledge such as this is certain and unshakeable. 'Be rooted and founded in love,' wrote St Paul. Just as the roots of trees hold the soil firm and stop erosion, so it is the roots of love that hold the ground of our being together. They provide the context in which we live and grow. And they each trace back to God as the first root of all being. The roots of love in our life bring us into context with him, with ourselves and with each other. And they show us that to be is to be in connection, each contributing to the other.

Sanity and balance mean knowing the context in which we live. This form of knowledge makes us sensitive to the presence of God in all our surroundings. Meditation teaches us in the only certain way, by experience, that his presence is not external to us. It is interior, the presence that makes up and holds together the ground of our being. So we come no longer to *look* for God's presence in the externals of our life but to *recognize* him in them because our eyes are opened interiorly to his indwelling Spirit. We no longer try to grasp hold of God, to possess him. Rather we are grasped by his presence, interiorly and exteriorly, because we know that his presence is all pervasive and the ground of all that is.

To be possessed by God in this way is the only true freedom. The tyranny of love is the only true relationship. Inevitably we fear this as it develops or emerges during our pilgrimage, because our image of freedom is so different, so naïvely imagined as the freedom to do rather than to be. But if we have the courage to be simple and humble enough to enter this *real* freedom, then we discover in ourselves the power of a faith that is unshakeable. Christian confidence is the discovery of this unshakeability and it is this confidence that underlies Christian compassion, tolerance and acceptance. We are made wonderfully secure in our own existence by this discovery, and out of this security we are empowered to drop our defences and to go out to the other. Our faith is unshakeable, not rigid, because it is one with the ground of our being. Through Christ's union with his disciples his faith becomes their faith and their faith is not an adjunct to their being. It is the breath of their spirit's life.

So, deepening our commitment to this pilgrimage means deepening the knowledge that faith gives birth to in the soul. As Christ is formed in us, as we ourselves live no longer for ourselves but for him and as his spirit breathes the new life of faith into our mortal bodies, we do come to know Christ more deeply. Maybe it sounds arrogant to say we come to know Christ as we persevere in meditation. But the truth is not less than this. We come to know what it is to live every moment, every decision, joy or difficulty from within his presence and so out of the infinite resources of his power – the power of love and compassion, an unshakeable reality.

How do we enter this presence? How can we acquire this 'knowledge that is beyond knowledge'? Because it is the knowledge of unknowing, it is the presence that forms when we allow ourselves to go beyond being present merely to ourselves and instead become present to God – to be known and loved into full being by him. As we are unformed he is formed. We have to learn to forget ourselves. Nothing is simpler to do. It is the condition of full simplicity. Yet nothing – or so it seems – is more difficult for us. It is so easy in theory to accept this. But in practice it is so difficult to live and love as if the other were really more important than ourselves, or as if our first loyalty were really not to self but to the other.

The greatest difficulty is to begin, to take the first step, to launch out into the depth of the reality of God as revealed in Christ. Once we have left the shore of our own self we soon pick up the currents of reality that give us our direction and momentum. The more still and attentive we are, the more sensitively we respond to these currents. And so the more absolute and truly spiritual our faith becomes. By stillness in the spirit we move in the ocean of God. If we have the courage to push off from the shore we cannot fail to find this direction and energy. The further out we travel the stronger the current becomes, and the deeper our faith. For a while the depth of our faith is challenged by the paradox that the horizon of our destination is always receding. *Where are we going with this deeper faith?* Then, gradually we recognize the meaning of the current that guides us and see that the ocean is infinite.

Leaving the shore is the first great challenge, but it is only necessary to *begin* to face the challenge. Even though the challenges may become greater later, we are assured that we shall be given everything we need to face them. We begin by saying the mantra. Saying the mantra is always to be beginning, to be returning to the first step. We learn in time that there is only one step between us and God.

Opening our hearts to the spirit of Christ is the only way into the certain knowledge that that step has been taken. Christ has taken it in himself. He himself *is* the step between God and man because he is God and man. The language we use to express this mystery, the greatest and fundamental mystery of the human race and of all time, is pathetically inadequate – as the theological controversies down through the centuries have shown. No language or concept or metaphor can express the mystery of Christ, because Christ is the full embodiment of God and there can be no adequate expression of God except his own self-expression. The only way to know Christ is to

116

enter his personal mystery, leaving ideas and words behind. We leave them behind in order to enter the silence of full knowledge and love to which meditation is leading each of us.

A New Beginning

At about 8.45 a.m. on 30 December 1982 Father John took the last step of his pilgrimage. He died peacefully in the monastery with several of us around him.

Father John was buried at Mount Saviour Monastery on Monday, 3 January 1983, and a Memorial Mass was held in Montreal on 15 January at the Ascension of Our Lord Church, Westmount, where he and Father Laurence first stayed when they came to Montreal in 1977. Bishop Crowley was the principle concelebrant and the Benedictines from Mount Saviour and Weston Priory were present with us.

'The poverty and joy of our word leads us into the sea of the reality of God and, once there, it keeps us simply in the current of the Spirit and leads us to a place unknown to us where we know ourselves in Him, in His eternal now' (John Main's letter of June 1979). Father John's illness accelerated rapidly after he wrote his last newsletter, and his sudden decline in the last two weeks further prepared us for the mystery of his death. We faced this mystery from out of a strong paradox: the paradox of human sorrow and grief, the bitter loss of his warmth and humour, his strength and gentleness as part of our own ordinary life, his great inspiration and power of clarification and encouragement. Yet all this loss was permeated by the joy of knowing that he had passed through the single focal point of which he had so often spoken, and that he had begun the life of infinite expansion in the love of God for which his work among us prepared him. We felt his absence more deeply than ever before, and yet we had never felt him closer.

Those days were like the experience of the early Christians who wept and rejoiced for their dead and risen Lord. This was because we all die and rise in Christ, and if we are open to his presence in the Resurrection we must therefore be open to the presence of each other as members of his glorified body. In Christ we learn that love is stronger than death.

Over the previous few months there had been an extraordinary surge of witness to the profound effect Father John had on many peoples' lives. Everyone who had ever been open to his teaching was changed and enriched by his sharing of what he himself had received through his own absolute and courageous, simple and loving openness to the mystery which contains us all. His teaching was and is rooted in the mystery itself, and so it enjoys the life and unpredictable pattern of the mystery. His new life in the Kingdom means new life for the work he began.

We strive to be faithful to the gift his life and teaching gave to us and to so many.

Laurence Freeman OSB

Key to Letters

Bibliography of John Main's Writings

Word into Silence (London, Darton, Longman and Todd, 1980; New York, Paulist Press, 1981)
Letters from the Heart (New York, Crossroad , 1982)
Moment of Christ (London, Darton, Longman and Todd, 1984; New York, Crossroad , 1984)

Published by the Benedictine Priory of Montreal (also available from the Christian Meditation Centre, London):

Christian Meditation: The Gethsemani Talks (1977)
Christian Mysteries: Prayer and Sacrament (1979)
Death: The Inner Journey (1983)
The Hunger for Prayer (1983)
The Monastic Adventure (1983)
Monastic Prayer and Modern Man (1983)
The Other-Centeredness of Mary (1983)
Community of Love (1984)

Monastic Studies (1984) no. 15, devoted to the life and work of John Main, and the *Communitas* tapes by John Main are available from the Christian Meditation Centre, London, and the Benedictine Priory, Montreal (for addresses see p. vi).